"A fabulous book for managers and coaches. Successfully delivers the vision of simplicity of framework that recognizes adaptability of approach in changing mindset. The impact for our business has been significant.

Coaching is a critical skill for any people manager and there are many tools available. Often they are complex and give the sense that hours of preparation and coaching is needed for an impact or they are too simple and do not reflect the complexities of real life. This book offers a practical and simple framework to orient though coaching conversations, whilst recognising that different situations need a different approach. A great toolkit for any manager."

—Brooke Finlayson, Chief Learning Officer, Mondelez International

"Mining insights from thousands of coaching engagements, Conner and Hirani have brilliantly demystified the coaching process and uncovered the conversations that truly matter. Their book offers a powerful system that will help all coaches increase their relevance, multiply their impact, and enable others to be at their best when they need it most."

—Liz Wiseman, bestselling author of *Multipliers* and *Rookie Smarts*

"A very practical book on deepening coaching conversations by two very accomplished and thoughtful coaches, backed up by research and great case examples."

—Peter Hawkins, Professor of Leadership and Co-Author of
Systemic Coaching: Delivering Value Beyond the Individual
and author of *Leadership Team Coaching*

"This approach to coaching has fundamentally changed the Integrated Device Technology culture. As a result attrition is down and financial performance is up. I see leaders who have experienced this work changing their entire vocabulary and approach to their jobs. They are more thoughtful in their actions and much deeper in their thinking."

—David Shepard, CEO and Senior Executive, Semiconductor Sector

"Jerry and Karim redefined the art of coaching conversations with these Four Great Coaching conversations that transcend and transform. This book offers a path to master the technique and methodology, I am sure that this book will soon become a classic."

—Enrique Lopez, Author and Founder of Academia
Interamericana de Coaching

The Four Greatest Coaching Conversations is essential reading for any coach or leader wishing to expand their repertoire of coaching skills and to facilitate growth and transformation that lasts. Jerry Connor and Karim Hirani offer an impressive guide for coaches that is well grounded in theory and research, yet practical and full of how-tos. A resource anyone coaching would find invaluable."

—Tony Clitheroe, Exec Coach, PCC, ICF (International Coach Federation)
President 2014–2018, WA Branch Australasia Charter Chapter

"Pragmatic, robust and insightful...a great resource for managers looking to adopt a coaching style with their teams and for leaders wanting to nurture a coaching culture within their organisations."

—Abi Marchant, HRD Food Sector, 2011–2017

"This book brings a rich diversity and depth of background research, and combines it with wisdom harvested from vast amounts of collective practice to create an elegantly simple set of heuristics. It is accessible and eminently practical, while laying out natural sequences for guiding you through ever deeper layers of mastery in your coaching practice."

—Jonathan Reams, Associate professor, Norwegian
University of Science and Technology

"This book is deep yet easy to read. It is rigorous in the treatment of the data and with the wisdom of the practice of coaching that infers what is not easily apparent; it is ambitious without claiming to be 'the ultimate coaching approach'; it is exhaustive and written in the spirit of apprentice in the background. For a coach or manager, this will be of much value to you, your coaching practice and your leadership."

—Francisco Villalta, PCC, Senior Coach, author of *Nacemos con alas luego aprendemos a volar* (Amazon's Best Selling) and *Memorias de una rosa*

"At last, the secret is out! – a breakthrough guide for coaches and leaders alike. A must-read guide for coaches, managers and leaders who wish to use coaching conversations to skilfully cut through complexity to reach clarity and create fundamental change that lasts.

For the past decade I've used Jerry and Karim's four greatest conversations, with outstanding results. I love the fact that I can use this approach whilst maintaining the integrity of my own (personal) coaching style. By following the guidelines outlined in this book a coach or leader will feel extremely confident about creating fundamental change in both the mindset and behaviour of the coachee. It's about time the four greatest conversations were shared with the world!"

—Judy McGinn, PCC, Executive Coach, ICF Australasia Western Australia Branch Professional Development Team Coordinator and Facilitator

"Chalk full of research-based insights and practical tools to support changing one's underlying mindset in order to make sustainable behavioral change and overcome common leadership challenges. Changing our mindset is fundamental to sustainable behavioral change. This book provides the context, tools and research to do just that."

—Carmen T Acton, MBA, Co-Director Internal Programs, ICF San Francisco Bay Area Coaches

"I have been coached personally by Karim, and as a business we have worked with BTS Coach for 4 years with the frameworks and techniques in this book. The impacts of the Be and Relate shifts in particular have been significant for me, professionally and personally, and for other individuals as well as us as an organization. It's hard to capture the magic of a great coach in a book or other medium, but this book does a brilliant job of explaining these powerful ideas and practical ways to apply them."

—Jivan de Silver, Strategy Director UK Market, Global Hospitality/Leisure Business

"Most managers I coach admit that, despite their best intentions, they tend to revert to advising and problem solving, rather than coaching. *The Four Greatest Coaching Conversations* gives leaders practical examples of how to use the right coaching conversation when coaches need help to build confidence, connection, inspiration or to have their mindset challenged. Stories, tips and example coaching questions help readers make sense of and apply the ideas presented. Drawing on a combination of neuroscience and psychological theory, Connor and Hirani's book is a useful tool for managers to build their mastery in the core leadership practice of coaching."

—Dr. Vicki Webster, Incisive Leaders

"Karim and Jerry have captured the essence of coaching in this informative and instructive book. Their models are profound and are based both on extensive research and psychological theories getting to the heart of how coachees and organisations can meet their potential. They present these simply, illustrated by case studies and offer clear, step-by-step explanations as to how to use these in coaching conversations. The chapter on subpersonalities adds an additional perspective, which takes their models to a new dimension. The exceptional element in this book is the way they combine simplicity with depth and offer line managers and coaches an innovative way to help individuals, teams and organisations make profound changes in a short time. I think this will become a must for all of us who have coaching conversations."

—Keren Smedley, PCC, author of several books
including *Who's that Woman in the Mirror*

"This book, *The Four Greatest Coaching Conversations,* integrates coaching skills, presence and psychological theories perfectly, and is for people who want a higher level of coaching skills. It inspires me. If you want to improve your coaching proficiency and coach presence as a master, this will help you to deeply see the coachee more than the presenting issues and goals of the coachee. After reading this book, you will feel like you got a masters degree in coaching."

—Sabrina Park, PCC, APAC (Asia Pacific Alliance of Coaches)
President 2013–2015, Founder of 'Positive 100 Days
Project' movement for world peace

"This is a great book for anyone learning, or honing their skills, as a coach or as a line manager. Through a series of real-life examples, the authors provide a thought provoking and structured approach to coaching individuals who are open to transformational change. On the face of it, the model, tools and techniques are simple to use, and yet reach deep into the psyche of individuals, enabling them to achieve sustainable change."

—Kate O'Loughlin, Team and Leadership Coach,
The Talent Toolbox, author of *The Science of Talent: How to find, grow and keep the right people in your organisation*

"We all need to know why we do what we do and how to shift our thinking to create new behaviors and habits in a safe space to unlock our own potential and that of our organizations. Connor and Hirani's *The Four Greatest Coaching Conversations* are the keys to transforming employee motivation and productivity quickly and effectively – a must read for all professional coaches and leaders."

—Maria Newport, co-author of *3 Elements for Effective Recruiting: Preparation – Selection – On boarding* and Managing Principal of Newport O'Connor (Executive Coaching & Consulting)

The Four Greatest Coaching Conversations

Change Mindsets, Shift Attitudes, and Achieve Extraordinary Results

Jerry Connor and Karim Hirani

NICHOLAS BREALEY
PUBLISHING

BOSTON • LONDON

First published in 2019 by Nicholas Brealey Publishing
An imprint of John Murray Press

A Hachette UK company

24 23 22 21 20 19   1 2 3 4 5 6 7 8 9 10

A CIP catalogue record for this title is available from the British Library

Library of Congress Control Number: 2019946464

ISBN 978-1-5293-9106-0
US eBook 978-1-5293-9109-1
UK eBook 978-1-5293-9108-4

Printed and bound in the United States of America.

John Murray Press policy is to use papers that are natural, renewable, and recyclable
products and made from wood grown in sustainable forests. The logging and
manufacturing processes are expected to conform to the environmental regulations
of the country of origin.

John Murray Press Ltd   Nicholas Brealey Publishing
Carmelite House   Hachette Book Group
50 Victoria Embankment   53 State Street
London EC4Y 0DZ   Boston, MA 02109, USA
Tel: 020 3122 6000   Tel: (617) 263 1834

www.nbuspublishing.com

Contents

Acknowledgements

There are many people to acknowledge that have contributed to the ideas and refinements of the contents of this book. We would like to acknowledge and say thank you to:

Our associate coaches, who have learned, applied, refined and shaped these conversations through practice. We are proud of the work they do on themselves in authentically integrating these tools and applying them to truly transform their coachees and organizations. They are world class coaches, with feedback to be proud of!

Our colleagues and employees at BTS Coach. Our teams work tirelessly to allow our work in this book and beyond to make a difference in the world. There are so many to name here – we want to say thank you to each of you personally in your contribution to the success of the work we do so that we can touch the many.

Those who built, added and lead the way in expanding the work in multiple geographies and cultures including: Claire Provan, Danielle Marchant, Eleonora Golcher, Gayatri Das Sharma, Melissa Deroche, Nicola Palk, Paul Neville and Stephanie Peskett.

Our partners at Bridge who worked with us in cocreating some of the ideas shared in this book.

To BTS and their employees who have partnered with us to bring the magic of coaching to the work they do.

The contributors of the coaching and development profession – our theories and ideas are built on the 'shoulders of giants' and tap deeply into the great work of many great thought leaders in the world of coaching, transformation and change.

Our organizational clients who trust us to work within their organization to transform themselves in order to create a better planet and a better world, so that leaders can do the best work of their lives.

Our coachees who have taken ownership to become more self-aware in order to serve their organizations, family and society.

Those who have been alongside us in this journey for the longest: a special thankyou to Sue Stokely and Lee Sears who were there at the beginning and founded the business with Jerry. They had the courage and vision to take this work to new geographies and played a significant role in broadening and shaping our thinking. We are deeply grateful.

And of course, to our families, who have supported us, especially during the ups and downs of writing – thank you for your love and support. Thank you Rosie, Shehzma, Adie, Aila, Elliot, Kieran and Rayya.

The Four
Greatest Coaching
Conversations

Introduction

WHAT MAKES A GOOD COACH A GREAT ONE?
Imagine someone you know comes to you feeling really low. "The presentation bombed," she says, referring to a board-level presentation she'd been preparing for ages. "I'll never be taken seriously at that level."

How do you respond? Whether you have a coaching or line-manager relationship, how can you coach her? Does this kind of situation sound familiar?

As a coach it should make your ears perk up. It is a prime opportunity for one of the four great coaching conversations. It is a chance to help this person pick herself up after a difficult meeting and help her learn from this experience and emerge with new confidence in communicating her ideas. It is an opportunity to make a huge difference.

Most good coaches will recognize the chance to be helpful here by listening or offering some time to reflect on what happened—but great coaching is about more than this. Great coaches can turn this kind of situation into an opportunity to shift mindset, a sustainable way to create deep and lasting change in their coachees. That is because they know how to identify and use the four greatest coaching conversations. This common situation of responding to a setback is just one of them.

Discovering the Four Great Coaching Conversations

We started to identify these conversations based on some remarkable data. We are both founders and key leaders of BTS Coach. BTS Coach was the pioneer of affordable coaching, and the company manages around 300 coaches in more than 40 countries, coaching nearly 10,000 individuals a year. To manage quality, our coaches have always been asked to keep anonymized notes on their conversations.

By 2012 we realized that this data was a goldmine. Inadvertently, we had created a record of more than 100,000 conversations in which leaders were at their most open about the challenges they were struggling with and the insights that unlocked change. And, of course, what truly unlocked the change was mindset.

Each coachee was coming in with a live and critical challenge. In each situation, they needed to make a mindset shift in order to change. The power of this data was that through the conversations, we could track what the coaches were doing that created this shift.

Something fascinating emerged from this data. At the root of vastly different situations and scenarios, particular mindset shifts and certain conversations kept recurring. A leader who wants to influence peers, a line manager who wants to coach, or a salesperson who wants greater trust with customers may all need the same mindset shift to achieve their goal, and they may all need a similar conversation to help them.

We grouped our findings into four areas, each related to a mindset:

1. *"Be."* These were conversations about the individual's resourcefulness, confidence, and ability to stay calm, open, and empathetic in any situation. This included authenticity and being yourself when you most need it.

2. *"Relate."* These were conversations about relationships with other people. This included influencing, building trust, giving a difficult message, collaborating, or dealing with conflict.

3. *"Inspire."* These were conversations about direction, change, and purpose. This included responding proactively to situations of uncertainty, and knowing what you stand for and how to lead for it.

4. *"Think."* These were conversations about solving problems in a new way. This included identifying bias and seeking input from diverse sources, having creativity, strategy, innovation, and insight. This was about looking beyond the obvious.

These areas were pervasive. For example, a leader seeking coaching on public speaking and a leader seeking coaching on managing emotions might actually need the same thing when viewed through a mindset lens. In both cases the *Be* conversation would enable them to choose their attitude or state in critical situations.

Interestingly, the truly great coaches would pick this up and used the right tool for the right mindset. The critical coaching conversation with the individual who wanted to be more confident at public speaking followed the same path as the coaching intervention with the person who wanted to manage their emotions. If the shift is the same, the coaching approach is the same.

And, logically, if you need to match the conversation to the shift, the same technique will not work for *Relate*, *Inspire*, and *Think* shifts. In each case, if you want to change mindset, something very different is required.

These findings are remarkable. Let's explore further how the shifts are different and why this is important to understand.

Each shift is fundamental and creates a step change in performance. But each shift is different and requires the coach to work in a different way.

Take two examples:

One coachee was a talented marketer. In everyday business, her quality shone through. But when it came to "selling her strategies" to senior leaders or making the case for a course of action with critical peers, she was less effective. The coach focused on what we will discover are classic *Inspire* questions. He asked the coachee to shape her vision for the difference her strategies might make. He coached her to clarify the change she wanted to lead in the business and build a strong narrative to bring it to life for the board. But it still failed. Why? Because the coach was focusing on the wrong conversation. Our coachee did not lack a clear sense of purpose or the ability to shape a story. The issue here is one of resourcefulness in negotiation with senior leaders. The only way to really address this is with the *Be* conversation, which will help her understand why she is becoming defensive and losing authority with senior audiences, and help her respond at her best in these negotiations with senior leaders.

Another coachee was an entrepreneur. After early success, he was experiencing a series of losses. Naturally he was starting to question his business idea. In this case, the coach focused on the *Be* conversation. The coach helped the coachee understand the doubts that began to creep in with the constant failures. The coach then helped the coachee build new, more resourceful responses to enable the entrepreneur to bounce back from disappointment. But the business kept failing. In this case the need was not a *Be* one. It's critical for entrepreneurs to notice feedback their products receive in the market and to challenge the way they think about their business. This points to the heart of learning agility. Rather than helping the coachee become more resilient, the need here was to coach his assumptions about the business. This is a classic *Think* coaching need.

Each of these cases used the wrong coaching conversation, and the coaching ultimately did not create sustainable behavior change or results. There are many such stories in our data. We track impact by whether an individual experienced "significant change" in coaching. And there is a direct correlation between addressing the conversation the coachee is really talking about and the coachee making significant change.

But what does this mean for you as leader and coach?

You need to be able to identify and listen for clues as to which of the four great coaching conversations the coachee is seeking. The appropriate map for that conversation can then guide you. If you do this, your chances of helping your coachees make a sustained and significant change—a change in mindset—increase dramatically.

So what are they?

Put simply, the heart of the four conversations are (we will look at the underlying mindsets later):

1. The *Be* conversation, when someone is feeling lousy, unconfident or unresourceful

2. The *Relate* conversation, when someone needs to build trust or connection with others

3. The *Inspire* conversation, when someone can't inspire themselves or others with a clear purpose or direction

4. The *Think* conversation, when someone needs to find new ideas or creative solutions

Critically, they work beyond formal coaching sessions. Most leaders know that coaching needs to be responsive in the moment—you don't always have the luxury of a series of conversations around a long-term goal. A colleague may come to you and say, "I'm frustrated with my colleague after our meeting. Help." The beauty of these four conversations is that the ideas can be used in the moment, over a five-minute focused coaching conversation, or over a longer-term planned conversation around an objective.

Let's take each in turn.

Conversation 1: The Be Shift

When someone is feeling lousy, unconfident, or unresourceful

The example at the beginning of the chapter is typical of a *Be* conversation. We introduced a team member who was feeling low after a presentation to the top team. While the cause may be different, all human beings experience the need for this conversation every day. There are topics about which we are defensive, unsure, or anxious. Situations or people that don't bring out the best in us. No matter who you are coaching, you will find there are times when they aren't at their best. When they feel lousy, unconfident, or unresourceful about something.

Changing the way your coachees respond to situations like this can be transformational. The mindset change is to do with building their ability to be their best when they most need it, and therefore holds the key, for example, to being confident and authoritative with a senior audience, or calm and authentic in a difficult work situation.

The ubiquity of this conversation was highlighted in 2016 when we worked with Singapore Management University to analyze more than 900 coach/coachee interactions.[1] Each interaction covered at least four coaching sessions over a period of several months. Working independently, a doctoral student categorized these conversations according to *Be, Relate*, other, or a mix. The levels will be discussed in Part Three of this book. For now, focus on the areas in totality. Put the table above in between these two paragraphs.

The results show how significant *Be* and *Relate* conversations are to most leaders today. They are at the heart of emotional intelligence. In particular, the *Be* shift is the most common need expressed in North America and the second most common globally.

	Europe	Asia	North America
Be Level One	26%	10%	36%
Relate Level One	33%	36%	27%
Be Level Two	3%	1%	4%
Relate Level Two	7%	10%	8%
Others	31%	43%	25%
	100%	100%	100%

Conversation 2: The Relate Shift

When someone needs to build trust or connection with others

Here is a typical *Relate* situation:

> Imagine you lead a sales team. One of your top account executives has been trying to close a deal. Every one of the key decision makers in the customer business is on board except for one finance director. "I've tried everything," fumes your team member, "but he's so small minded. All he thinks about is cost. What can I do?"

How do you respond? How can you coach your team member to learn from this experience and emerge with a reconceived approach to influencing the finance director? How can they recognize their judgments and reactions, and shift the mindset toward others to greater understanding, empathy, and response?

Most coaches regularly encounter this situation, where people come to us for coaching in dealing with others.

In fact, according to research with Singapore Management University, this need is the most common one expressed in both the European and Asian samples, and it is the most common need across our data set.[2] This is not surprising. Success for most people depends on their ability to engage with, influence, and coach others. It sits at the core of leadership. And it is often the one element that most defines effectiveness.

We will explore the *Relate* conversation in more depth—and how to help the account executive—in chapter 2.

Conversation 3: The Inspire Shift

When someone can't inspire themselves or others with a clear purpose or direction

Here is a typical *Inspire* situation:

> Imagine you are coaching a high performer. She has been working flat out over the past year and has exceeded all her targets. But she is exhausted and starting to get feedback from others that she is overly driven and not inspirational. She opens up to you, sharing that she's starting to wonder whether it's all worth it, and she needs some support to reignite her inspiration.

How do you respond? How would you coach her? How can you help her discover what is really important to her and how to lead in a way that is inspiring to her and those around her?

This kind of conversation is becoming much more prevalent in the modern world. In generations past, success was typically defined by pursuing a well-defined career and completing defined tasks to certain levels. It was less important to know what you wanted, nor to chart your own course. Now people are expected to "own their own careers," to "lead in uncertainty," and to create their own vision for success. This conversation is core to coaching others in this area.

As a coach it's a brilliant mindset changing conversation to coach people who want clarity on who they want to be and the change they want to lead. It's one of our favorites.

We'll explore this conversation and how to coach the "marketer" in chapter 3.

Conversation 4: The Think Shift

When someone needs to find new ideas or creative solutions

A typical *Think* situation might look like this:

> Imagine a factory manager comes to you for support. He has been challenged to increase efficiency and cut costs. The ideas generated so far feel stale. He wants some support to "get out of this rut."

How do you respond? How can you coach him to think differently and hence to create genuinely breakthrough ideas? The *Think* conversation addresses this, as well as how we create and innovate new solutions.

This conversation is *not* about giving people new ideas or creative solutions. That wouldn't be coaching. It *is* about challenging thinking. It is about coaching to view a situation through new and different lenses, unleashing new levels of creativity and innovation in the coachee. This shift enables some people to step back from a situation and pick out the root cause, to create strategic insight and develop radically new ideas.

It is about recognizing habitual thinking, such as, "how I or we normally think about this," and consciously moving beyond these assumptions to create new ways of looking at it. It's about getting curious again.

In Summary – the Four Greatest Coaching Conversations

The Four Greatest Conversations	When do you use this conversation?	How might it help your coachees?
The *Be* conversation	When someone is feeling lousy, unconfident, or unresourceful	Being at their best when they most need it, confidence, resilience, emotional control, resourcefulness, having a growth mindset
The *Relate* conversation	When someone needs to build trust or connection with others	Influencing others, giving difficult messages, listening, building relationships with those they find challenging, overcoming conflict
The *Inspire* conversation	When someone can't inspire themselves or others with a clear purpose or direction	Leading in uncertainty, setting direction, clarity, knowing what they stand for, meaning and values
The *Think* conversation	When someone needs to find new ideas or creative solutions	Creativity, problem solving, strategic insight, challenging the way things are done, coming up with breakthrough ideas, innovation

The Secret Behind the Four Greatest Coaching Conversations

So why are these conversations so important? What is the secret behind them? Why did they stand out so strongly in our data? We found that these four conversations are so critical because they work on mindset. This means the change they unlock is deeper, longer lasting, and more significant. This is because mindset is at the heart of behavior change.

To bring it to life, consider this scenario, which may sound familiar to you:

> You receive more feedback that a member of your team is frustrating his colleagues with his poor communication and lack of sensitivity. You are unsure what to do. You have given him this feedback on several previous occasions, and he's committed to changing. You've sat down and shaped a development goal to this effect. You had some great coaching conversations, but he still isn't changing.

Why not? And how come all those carefully crafted coaching skills aren't working?

It's because these conversations do not strike at the turning point for change. A good conversation is not enough. We know this ourselves—think about the New Year's resolutions that fail or the commitments to better ourselves that never end up coming to fruition. Behavior change takes more than good intention. It requires a change in mindset. In the above example, the team member will not change his behavior until we address the mindset. To do this, let's look at mindset.

What do we mean by changing mindset?

A close friend had a heart bypass operation when he was 56. It was necessitated by high cholesterol. The specialist advised him to alter his lifestyle to avoid a repeat. In spite of good intentions, he failed to substantially change his lifestyle, and sadly he died of heart disease five years later.

Why didn't he change? He had all the knowledge and skills he needed. He most certainly had the motivation. In fact, my friend is not unusual. According to one study, only one in seven people manage to change despite being told by a doctor that they have a condition that will threaten their life if they don't change.[3]

Or take a business situation. In 2007 Apple launched the iPhone. At the time, BlackBerry was the dominant player in the market. For the next four years BlackBerry's sales grew, and it continued to ignore the danger from its smaller competitor. BlackBerry executives couldn't see how users would abandon their keyboards for touchscreen technology. As a result, BlackBerry neither adapted nor changed, and it is now a fraction of the size of Apple.

Or take this behavioral example. According to research, 65 percent of employees in North America want more feedback.[4] So, it should be easy to persuade managers to give it, right? Far from it. Time and time again, we find that giving feedback is one of the behaviors managers find most difficult and generally avoid. But why, especially when people clearly want it?

In each of these cases, change is not happening. My friend didn't change his lifestyle even though it was in his interest to do so. BlackBerry did not challenge their views of the market, even though they remained market leader for a few more years and had plenty of time to respond. Managers are not changing their views on giving feedback to team members, even though we know employees want feedback.

In each case telling people to change isn't enough. Nor is it enough to simply come up with good coaching intentions, ask coaching questions, or give them models and tools to improve. There is something else at stake. That something is mindset.

Mindsets are the beliefs, assumptions, and mental frames—often unconscious—that shape people's actions. If our coachee is unaware of mindsets, they may find that their good intentions to change lapse in the face of stress, and then old habits kick in. Mindsets have corresponding physiological and emotional components.

Recent advances in neuroscience help explain this. We learn that the frequent firing of neurons in the brain create deep pathways, or "rivers of thinking." The good news is that brains are "plastic," and these pathways can be changed. The bad news is that new connections will have to be built to do this.

But without creating new connections, natural reactions will be defined by these established neural pathways. So, our coachee's mindset—either their new one, or their old one—will play a key role in driving their behavoir—either their new one or their old one—which in turn drives their impact and results. In the three examples above, unlocking the mindset that drove the behavior would have been key to my friend changing his diet, BlackBerry facing the challenge of Apple, and persuading managers to give feedback.

Let's take another simple example to illustrate the impact of changing mindset on behavior.

If a manager believes that negative feedback will upset an employee and leave them unmotivated, then the manager will probably hold back on giving the feedback. Even if the manager does try to give feedback in spite of their belief, it may not work. Say for example the manager attends a feedback skills workshop and returns with a new feedback model. They try it on their employee. But because they believe that giving negative feedback will upset their employee, they are anxious when they give it. In their anxiety the message comes across more bluntly and more aggressively than they intended, skewing the truth of the message. The employee picks up the anxiety together with the clumsy message and does, in fact, become upset.

The manager's mindset (negative feedback will upset the employee) has meant that trying to adopt a new behavior on its own didn't work—and in fact backfired, reinforcing the original mindset.

Mindset Drives Behavior Drives Results

"Your beliefs become your thoughts, your thoughts become your words, your words become your actions, your actions become your habits, your habits become your values, your values become your destiny." (A quotation attributed to Mahatma Gandhi)

By contrast, suppose the manager recognized they held this belief or assumption that feedback will upset their employee (notice the certainty of the assumption—it "will") and was able to change it with the *Be* conversation. Perhaps they replaced the belief that "feedback will upset my employee" with a belief that "my employee would love to know how they are doing." In this scenario, the results would be different. The manager can now give the feedback with confidence. They will therefore be free of anxiety and hence able to deliver the message clearly and with care. And, of course, the result will be different. Mindset drives behavior, and behavior drives results. This is expressed well by A.J. Crum, P. Salovey, and S. Achor, who define a mindset as "a mental frame or lens that selectively organizes and encodes information, thereby orienting an individual toward a unique way of understanding an experience and guiding one toward corresponding actions and responses."[5] It has been repeatedly confirmed by authors such as A.B. Frymier and N.K. Nadler.[6]

As we go through each conversation, we will refer to research that shows the impact of changing the mindset on business results. This works.

So, a great coach needs to coach with an awareness of mindset.

In fact, because coaching involves adult learning and growth, it is rarely simply about transmitting information or imparting new skills. Usually we are coaching others to learn to expand perspective, or change the way they look or respond. In other words, to change mindset.

We often hear, "Well, if they had a better attitude they would succeed," or, "They just need to change their outlook." But no one provides the answer to actually do that—change the attitude, outlook, or mindset. This book will show you how we have successfully worked with others to do this, thousands of times.

As coaches, we need to master the art and science of coaching to transform mindset. By doing this we can truly help coachees grow and change. It is a science in the sense the below-the-surface workings of the four conversations have been researched and tested. It is an art because every human being is different—each response to the questioning in the four conversations will be different, each insight for the coachee will be different, and each real-life application will be different.

We will help you identify when each of the four conversations is needed and how to have them. You don't need to have any coach training to use them, but if you have had formal training, the conversations should complement it.

This book is written in that light. Everything discussed in the following pages and the four conversations are all about changing mindset. Changing mindset is the power of the four conversations.

This book goes beyond foundational coaching models you may have come across, like GROW, listening, or asking questions. This book will

Note on coaching methodology: does our approach align with coaching professions, such as the International Coach Federation or European Mentoring and Coaching Council?

We believe it does.

While this book is aimed at line managers and the coaching all of us can do every day, these conversations could take place in the context of a professional coaching intervention, i.e., one that has a coaching ethical framework, with a coaching contract, and in service to the objective of the client. Many coach trainings will offer tools/models/processes from Neuro-Linguistic Programming or teach models about the gremlin or critic in our minds to support our coachees. What we are adding to the field is other models, researched theory, and frameworks that shed more light on the territory of experience. This adds to the power of noticing what the coachee is really talking about, and it provides focus on the mindset change that will drive the goal.

This means we can listen with greater attunement, ask more powerful questions, offer direct awareness/insight, and provoke lasting change. In coaching mindsets we will still be listening, asking questions, creating awareness—but with the wisdom of the four great conversations behind us.

We feel these models contribute significantly to the coaching process.

With transparent contracting and aligning the conversation with the coachee's goal, these tools can be adapted to be powerful in professional coaching.

help you to understand mindset, truly listen for the right conversation, and ask powerful questions by leveraging the tools and process to change it. This will enhance any approach to having great coaching conversations.

You will discover a shortcut into simple, proven, transformational ways to shift the mindset in each of the four conversations, giving you the ability to have a genuinely transformative impact when your coachee most needs it.

Are the impacts of these conversations proven?

Because we coach at volume, we are arguably the first coaching business to be able to use "big data," and to test and refine its approach. We have always believed in transparency and openly share our methodology with coachees before their coaching. We believe this means we can go deeper, faster. And the results support this. Our NPS (net performance score) is 98 percent, and more than 97 percent of our coachees claim to have made changes as a result of the coaching. Most significantly, the number of coachees who claim that the change is significant and lasting (an indicator of mindset change) is correlated to the coach picking and using the relevant conversation for each coachee.

Why is this important? Because every tool shared in this book will have been tested and refined with thousands of coachees. You will be tapping into the insight from thousands and thousands of coaching hours and hundreds of coaches. And we'll be sharing those tools that have maximum impact, supported by data.

Furthermore, we will also show how our four areas are the most relevant ones in today's world by sharing research from thought leaders in the areas of leadership and development. They highlight the same four areas! We will discuss the business or organizational impact for each of the four conversations. For those who like more insight, we will share how these four mindsets relate to human psychological development.

How to Read this Book

This book is divided into three sections.

Part One: The Four Greatest Coaching Conversations

This section brings the four conversations to life. Each chapter takes a conversation and helps you understand it, experience it, and discover how to coach others. We suggest going through the theory to understand the concepts and then working through the reflective exercises at the end of the chapter with your own examples to really live it. The more you have experienced it yourself, the more you will be able to authentically support someone else in these great conversations. At the end of each section you will find additional hints and tips on how to successfully work with the insights when coaching others.

Part Two: Organizations Have Mindsets Too

In chapter 5 we'll look beyond coaching individuals and explore the way organizations and teams can be considered to have mindsets too—and how the four conversations can help solve business challenges.

Part Three: Going Deeper: Understanding Mindset Change

In chapters 6, 7, and 8, we'll move from the practical to the theoretical and give a little more depth and analysis to the research and thinking behind this work. Is there genuinely a psychological difference between the conversations? What are the principles behind changing mindset? We will look at the psychology behind these conversations and how to master coaching others to change mindset. In the final chapter, we'll look beyond the four great conversations and give you a glimpse of how these conversations expand as your coachees become more mature and sophisticated.

For the purpose of simplicity, we refer to anyone using coaching skills with others in the workplace as a coach, whether as a leader having a development intervention, as a line manager having a great conversation, or as a professional coach. The person being coached will be referred to as the coachee.

Chapter **1**

Be

APPLYING THE BE CONVERSATION

    Application to other situations

    The business impact

    Practicing and applying it to yourself

    Applying it in coaching: other great coaching questions

    Hints and tips to shift from in the box to out of the box

SUMMARY

Understanding and Identifying the Conversation

Introduction

When someone is feeling lousy, unconfident, or unresourceful

In the introduction, we posed this scenario:

> Imagine someone you know comes to you feeling really low. "The presentation bombed," she says, referring to a board-level presentation she'd been preparing for ages. "I'll never be taken seriously at that level."

How do you respond? How can you coach her so that she can learn from this experience and come out of the conversation with new confidence communicating at this level?

In this chapter we'll explore the answer.

The Be conversation lies at the heart of personal effectiveness. It is one of the most fundamental coaching conversations. It will enable you to help others be at their best when they most need it. It is so often the key to unlocking a new level of performance in your coachees. At the same time, it will enable you to help them navigate life's challenges in a resilient and resourceful way.

Let's picture more details from this example. Imagine this person is a high-performing marketer who is articulate, bright, and really knows her stuff. But she keeps getting feedback that she lacks executive presence. When she presents to the top team or senior clients, she loses her spark and tightens up, coming across as wooden and tentative. Why is this? Why can't her intelligence and personality come out when she presents to senior leaders?

A simple metaphor might help.

A lady sat in front of a window. As she looked out, she began feeling frustrated. "Phil," she called to her husband, "look at the new neighbor next door. She is putting out dirty washing. This is wrong."

Phil simply replied, "Yes, dear."

The next morning, the lady shouted out again, this time more annoyed than before. "Phil, she's doing it again! I can't believe the guile of the woman. To put out dirty washing again. She is ruining my environment and the lovely view out of my window. She was starting to feel distressed, which was affecting her mood and her relationship.

"Yes, dear," Phil replied again.

This went on for a few days, only each time her stress levels increased further. Then something changed. "Phil, come here, quick!" she called. Phil ran over. "Look, the neighbor has put out clean washing. Finally! She has clearly learned the error of her ways. Someone has obviously talked to her. Now I can finally relax. Still, I can't believe what's wrong with the neighbor—I won't be smiling at her anytime soon."

Phil looked wry and hesitantly said, "Darling, um, I forgot to tell you. This morning I cleaned your window."

This story illustrates a fundamental idea at the heart of this shift: often, it is not the circumstances that are the source of stress, it is the "window" through which our coachees look—the window of their perception. When it is tarnished with unhelpful beliefs about the situation, they lose their resourcefulness and are less resilient. Their beliefs, assumptions, emotional patterns, and fears are making their window murky.

With the marketer, it is not the content or the act of presenting that is the challenge. She can do both. It is the "window" she is looking through, which makes her anxious about impressing senior leaders. Because she sees senior presentations as stressful occasions, she becomes anxious and doesn't shine. But her internal beliefs are driving this, not the situation itself.

The Be conversation is all about cleaning the window. *The mindset shift is about enabling people to see the situation clearly, free from fears and judgments, and to be fully resourceful in their response.*

When do we use this conversation?

For most of us it's obvious when someone is feeling lousy, unconfident, or unresourceful about something. We see it all the time.

The common thread here is these are all situations in which the coachee has the knowledge and skills they need but can't use them effectively. At their best they could handle the situation differently. The coaching focuses on the coachee finding their best self. They will quickly become far more effective.

What a coachee might say

An individual's self-talk is a sure sign that they aren't resourceful. Here are some examples.

- If you hear your coachee saying "I can't," or "There is no point in…," or "That won't work"
- (More subtle to pick up) If you feel your coachee is driven to achieve a particular outcome and starts using language like, "We must," or "We can't fail," then their relationship to the task at hand is likely to be fear based and they won't be fully resourceful

Figure 1-1: Be topics and challenges

- Coachees who express fearful thoughts: "If I do this, then XYZ will happen," "If I make a mistake in this area, then no one will forget it," or, "I can't afford to mess this one up"

- Coachees who take on too much responsibility: "I must," "I should," or "I ought to" are giveaway language

- Coachees who do the right thing and don't pay attention to their own needs

- Coachees who judge themselves or others: "I can't do this," "They are lazy," "I should have challenged them sooner," or "I'm not good enough"

Essentially, you will notice the exaggerated and dramatic assumptions that cloud their experience of what they are facing.

The other cue in what they say (sometimes nonverbally) is the coachee's feelings. If they are stressed, visibly upset, emotionally distant, or overwhelmed, this is a good cue to see if the Be conversation is relevant.

How to recognize the shift in this conversation

At its core, the Be coaching conversation empowers the coachee to respond at their best no matter what the situation. It will be most valuable to a coachee who can see a pattern of behavior that they can overturn. Here are some examples.

- A coachee who has resolved to listen more, but gets impatient and takes over when the pressure is on
- A coachee who goes quiet and doesn't express their ideas effectively in senior meetings
- A coachee who resolves to do something but loses confidence in the face of setbacks

In other words, by learning to shift their state and be more resourceful, they can change a behavior or achieve a goal that is otherwise eluding them. It can also help them respond to a recurring but challenging situation in a far more effective way.

The Be Conversation

A sample conversation in action

So let's see the Be conversation in full. We'll do this by going back to the case study we introduced both in the introduction and at the beginning of this chapter. How might a great coach help the marketer after her board presentation?

When she comes in after the unsuccessful presentation, she asks for some coaching support. The coach agrees.

COACH: *When did it start to go wrong for you?*

COACHEE: *Pretty early on—they were running late, and as I came in the CEO said, "We are short on time; can we keep this tight?"*

Part One (the Emotions stage)

COACH: *Take yourself back to the moment: how did you feel when he said this?*

COACHEE: *I felt quite anxious.*

COACH: *What were you telling yourself? What was your self-talk in that moment?*

COACHEE: *I was telling myself, "I have to get this right. Otherwise they'll keep writing me off."*

COACH: *And if that's true, then what does that mean about you?*

COACHEE: *I'm no good in these pressure situations.*

Part Two (the Truth stage)

COACH: *I wonder how we might be able to take a step back and see things from a different mindset, a different perspective that might be more truthful.*

COACHEE: *Yes.*

COACH: *Take a moment to breathe and connect with a time when you were feeling great. Now, connected to this moment, is it true that you "have to get it right"?*

COACHEE: *Probably not, but I do want to improve my impact with the board.*

COACH: *And do they "write you off"?*

COACHEE: *No, I guess not. They probably don't have a strong point of view. It is my job to shape this.*

COACH: *What's the truth to the statement that "I am no good in these pressure situations"?*

COACHEE: *Well, I wasn't great in this one, but sometimes—for example with a difficult customer—I focus on them, not me, and can be great under pressure.*

Part Three (the Conscious Choice stage)

COACH: *So we know that no single presentation is all or nothing, that you want to improve your impact with the board, and that you can be brilliant under pressure, especially when you focus on the other person, not yourself. How might you handle the next presentation differently?*

COACHEE: *I guess I could consciously focus on them. Maybe ask some questions and engage them first—like I would with a customer. And enjoy the situation. Take the pressure off myself and be the way I would with a customer.*

COACH: *And do you have another presentation coming up to try this?*

COACHEE: *Yes, as it happens, I am presenting to the same group next week. I'll use it as a chance to try my new approach.*

This is the Be conversation in action. Through the coaching, the coachee has turned a negative experience into a learning one, with a clear choice for the next situation.

Breaking the conversation down at high level: the ETC process

A quotation attributed to Carl Jung says,

"The most important question anyone can ask is: what myth am I living?"

In other words, what window am I looking through and living from?

The tool for coaching Be is a three-step process. It is based on three principles:

- The heart of the Be shift is recognizing that the lens through which our coachee looks determines their state and response; the events outside do not. It is a fundamental turning of perception—from thinking that life outside causes them to feel bad, to seeing instead that it is their own mindset or worldview. The lens through which they see the world truly drives their experience.

- This lens includes thoughts, beliefs, and assumptions with corresponding feelings and physiological patterns. We call these thoughts self-talk, voices, or thought patterns that—when our coachee is not at their best—will be negative, exaggerated, and dramatic. We will call this state "in the box." When "out of the box," our coachee's frame or mindset is more truthful and realistic.

- Our coachee's self-talk and feelings shape their behavior and impact. For example, when they aren't confident, they will often have self-doubting thoughts (*I am not good enough, I am not worthy*), which lead to feelings of insecurity or shyness. When they are unsure, they will often have worrying thoughts (*this is going to turn out badly,* or *something awful will happen*) with corresponding feelings of fear or anxiety.

To break free, these three steps of ETC are critical:

E – Emotion. Invite the coachee to notice the moment when they stop being resourceful, becoming aware of the feelings, physiology (e.g., butterflies in the stomach, sweating, etc.), and self-talk that drive their experience. This is fundamental because they are bringing awareness to their limiting mindsets and making them conscious. This allows their conscious mind to check them out.

T – Truth. Now metaphorically the coachee can clean their window by challenging and letting go of the limiting mindset, and access a more truthful and realistic mindset. We call this mindset the realist. What is true in response to the dramatic assumptions our coachee has believed? And what do they want?

C – Choice. Given this, how can they respond to the situation in a resourceful way?

Done well, this is potentially the most powerful tool to change aspects of behavior and impact. Let's explore each of these in more depth and look at the tools that will help in your coaching. We will focus on resourcefulness and share other applications of this conversation later in the chapter.

Breaking the conversation down at a high level: the coaching insights and models

Step One: Emotion (and Thought)

What is the purpose of this step?

Coaching to notice the moment they stop being resourceful and become aware of the underlying feelings and self-talk.

Why is this important?

This is fundamental because you are taking unconscious thoughts and making them conscious. In other words, the coachee is becoming aware of the filters on the window they look through. This allows them to release the mindset, enabling the conscious mind to check out their self-talk in the second step—Truth.

Critical Models and Insights

1. In and out of the box: To become conscious of the states that are unresourceful (in the box), and resourceful (out of the box). The first

part of the E step is awareness. Most people know when they are deeply unresourceful. But the trick to mastering the Be conversation is to become mindful of *all* the times resourcefulness drops and hence able to pick up on the more subtle clues. For example, picking up light tension sooner is much more effective than waiting for stress to accumulate.

2. Triggers: To facilitate understanding of the triggers—the critical turning point when our coachee goes in the box.

3. Self-talk: To notice self-talk, emotions, and physiology of the in-the-box mindset, and to understand the pessimistic and judgmental nature of the self-talk.

In and Out of the Box

Picture this situation: it's Monday morning. The coachee opens their mailbox and sees an email marked "urgent" from their boss. How might they respond?

Response A: They feel anxious, their heart sinks, and they think, "Oh, no—this is going to be bad. What have I done or what will this mean? This is an awful start to the week."

And guess what? Their expectations are likely to be self-fulfilling. With this mindset, the coachee is likely to be moody or distracted with colleagues. Perhaps their anxiety comes across in their meeting with their manager, and the meeting starts off on the wrong foot.

This is the state of **in the box**: the thoughts are dramatic; they are not feeling creative or open.

Response B: They feel unperturbed and wonder what is important to their manager. They also feel open and curious. Thoughts are something like: "This could be good news; I wonder what is urgent and how I can provide support."

This is the state of being **out of the box**: the coachee is feeling open, curious, and alive.

In both situations, the situation is the same—but a coachee can respond from an in-the-box or out-of-the-box mindset.

How does a coachee know if they are in the box or out of the box?

First, the feelings are different. This is the easiest way to work out which of the two emotional states they are in. As you can see, the feelings associated with the two states are very different.

There are subtleties in this model of which you need to be aware. If a coachee is simply feeling okay, then it is unlikely that they are truly out of the box. They can be drifting along in life and, while the lid is not firmly down on the box, they are still inside it. This is one to be careful about. In this state, the coachee has lowered their expectations of themselves and the world around them. They never really respond in a truly energized way with a sense of possibility. In business, driven, task-focused behavior is often mistaken for being out of the box. What we are looking to create here are those genuine out-of-the-box moments when the coachee feels truly alive and energized.

Closely connected to feelings is physiology. A coachee can notice their state of in the box or out of the box by observing their physiology. In the box, for example, they may experience their heart racing, butterflies

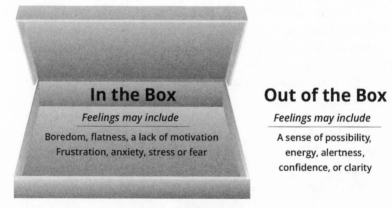

In the Box

Feelings may include

Boredom, flatness, a lack of motivation
Frustration, anxiety, stress or fear

Out of the Box

Feelings may include

A sense of possibility,
energy, alertness,
confidence, or clarity

Figure 1-2: In and out of the box

in the stomach, or tension. When out of the box, they may feel lighter, have relaxed muscles, or be smiling.

What is the impact of going in the box?

When a coachee is in the box, the impact is immediate and huge. At times it affects their behavior. Consider this example.

> *One coachee, Mr. Ortiz, had a woman on his team who never seemed to take the initiative. He realized that she was probably low in confidence, having had her role successively reduced by previous leaders. He resolved to build her confidence and encourage her gradually to take on more and more. He therefore invited her into a meeting. She arrived late, and her first words were, "I'm not sure what this is all about but I assume it's going to add to my workload." Mr. Ortiz's frustration immediately bubbled to the surface—and while he remained polite, his response of, "Well, maybe it would help if you didn't see new opportunities as threats" set the tone for a fruitless debate. Rather than building her confidence, he ended up trying to prove to her that her attitude was wrong.*

At other times, though, it is easy to assume that a person can "control" their response. Unfortunately, this is rarely the case. A significant amount of meaning in our communications comes from our nonverbal communications. In fact, when a person is saying one thing and actually feeling another, up to 90 percent of the impact of what they are saying comes from their nonverbal communication (body language and tone) and as little as 10 percent from their words.[1] If a coachee is in the box, they may try and convey with their words that they are not in the box. But in reality, the signals they give show otherwise. Other people almost invariably pick up an in-the-box state from these cues. As a result, leading from inside the box almost never has the intended impact, even if they try to "get a grip" and lead effectively.

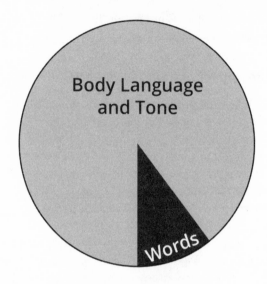

Figure 1-3: Body language and tone

A coachee can be in the box or out of the box about any situation they face in business. In fact, in our experience, most people in leadership roles experience a rollercoaster of in- and out-of-the-box moments throughout their day. One minute they can feel great, and the next minute their energy is on the floor. What happens to them?

The Trigger

A trigger is an event or situation that occurs prior to going in the box. It may be a big thing (e.g., some bad news) or a little thing (e.g., an unenjoyable task). The trigger moment is critical—before a coachee moves from one state to another, there will be a trigger.

The important thing is that, on many occasions, even when a coachee starts off full of energy, something then happens, and their mindset or state changes. They lose their spark and often with it their sense of possibility and perspective. Often the trigger event takes the form of a split-second moment that changes their state—for example, receiving an email or phone call. It is not easy to notice how often moods or thoughts alter in such moments, and the coachee ends up in the box.

When coaching it is useful to identify this moment. It helps our coachees understand what is going on within them and find their way back outside the box.

In the split second when they are "hit" by a trigger event, they will have thoughts (self-talk) about the situation that affect their feelings and physiological reactions. This affects the way they behave, the impact they have, and the results they achieve.

When the trigger occurs and they go in the box, the behavior becomes less than their best. Learning to notice when this happens is a key leadership skill.

Science journalist and author Daniel Goleman describes how our minds respond in the box. Our amygdala is situated in our temporal lobe and, among other things, is responsible for our fight-or-flight response. In other words, when triggered, the emotional response takes over and it shuts down abilities in the cortex (which explains why it's hard to think clearly—the "window" of perception is clouded). This is an evolutionary response that enables human beings to respond quickly—without

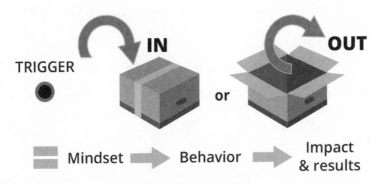

Figure 1-4: The trigger

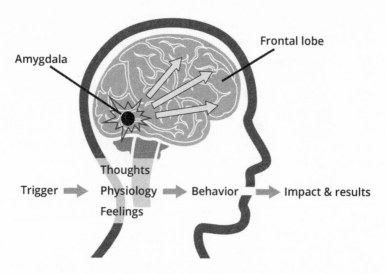

Figure 1-5: Amygdala hijack

waiting for conscious thought about danger. Goleman termed this the "amygdala hijack."[2] The triggered mindset has taken over.

But for most people, this is rarely helpful. They aren't often in physical danger, and most of the threats people face are better dealt with from a resourceful out-of-the-box state rather than through fight, flight, or freeze.

Self-talk: The Pessimist and the Judge

When a coachee looks at thoughts or self-talk associated with the in-the-box mindset, they are likely to notice two voices.

The Pessimist

The Pessimist immediately focuses in on the downsides of any given situation. The Pessimist may, for example, say, "Nothing I do will make a

Figure 1-6: The Judge and Pessimist

difference here," or immediately begin to see the downsides or problems associated with a given situation.

The Pessimist can be present in all situations.

The Judge

The Judge makes broad sweeping judgments of the situation or people involved. Sometimes these are aimed outward as the Judge attaches broad labels to other people or things. Most likely, the Judge also judges themselves or their actions.

The Judge can also be present every time they are in the box. The Judge often resides a bit deeper in the subconscious.

How was this shown in the example conversation?

The coach did this by first asking the coachee how she felt. This is to help the coachee realize she is in the box and to help her reveal her negative feelings and thoughts.

COACH: *Take yourself back to the moment, how did you feel when he said this?*

COACHEE: *I felt quite anxious.*

The coach then asked the coachee to express her Pessimist and Judge self-talk. Then, the coach probed a little to discover the big fear the coachee was holding.

COACH: *What were you telling yourself? What was your self-talk in that moment?*

COACHEE: *I was telling myself, "I have to get this right. Otherwise they'll keep writing me off."*

COACH: *And if that's true, then what does that mean about you?*

COACHEE: *"I'm no good in these pressure situations."*

Step Two: Truth

What is the purpose of this step?

For the coachee to metaphorically clean their window or challenge their mindset. What is true and what is dramatic?

Why is this important?

At the heart of shifting the mindset is to distinguish between fact truth and self-talk, which then allows the coachee to identify what is important in the situation. Effectively, you are coaching the coachee to challenge the limiting mindset and to access a more conscious, truthful, and realist mindset. This will allow your coachee to see the situation from a clearer "window" or mindset.

Critical models and insights

The Realist is another voice that challenges the assumptions of the pessimistic and judgmental self-talk. It is the voice of reality. The Realist finds the truth or value that is most important in the situation.

The Realist

The Realist is the key to getting out of the box. This involves accessing the mindset from the conscious self, rather than being caught by the lower-self mindsets, with their pessimistic and judgmental thoughts. Our Pessimist and our Judge are so powerful because they are extremely dramatic. The Judge tends to make sweeping statements like "He is lazy" or "She is not a people person." The Pessimist tends to be melodramatic, with "This is not going to work" or "I'll never get recognized here."

All dramatic statements are false. This is not to say that some people aren't lazy some (and perhaps most) of the time, but no one is lazy in every situation. Unfortunately, our brains cannot easily distinguish the dramatic from the real, so while you are listening to your Pessimist or

Figure 1-7: The Realist

Judge, your brain believes these generalizations to be true, without questioning them, and they therefore affect the way you feel. Your limiting beliefs or mindsets then become self-fulfilling.

The Realist Tells Us the Truth

Our Realist is the part of the coachee that is able to tell the truth. It distinguishes the dramatic from the truth. It allows the coachee to be clear and more honest about what is going on in the world. The Realist arises when the coachee is out of the box—it sees things with greater clarity and truth, rather than the pessimistic and judgmental aspect of the self-talk.

It is important to note that the Realist is not the same as positive thinking. The Realist is about balanced truth.

So how did this work in our example conversation?

First the coachee was invited to access their Realist.

> COACH: *I wonder how we might be able to take a step back and see from a different mindset, a different perspective that might be more truthful.*

> COACHEE: *Yes.*

> COACH: *Take a moment to breathe and connect with a time when you were feeling great.*

Then the coach played back the Pessimist and Judge statements—using the coachee's own words—and asked if they were true.

> COACH: *Now, connected to this moment, is it true that you "have to get it right"?*

> COACHEE: *Probably not, but I do want to improve my impact with the board.*

> COACH: *And do they "write you off"?*

> COACHEE: *No, I guess not. They probably don't have a strong point of view. It is my job to shape this.*

COACH: *What's the truth to the statement that "I am no good in
these pressure situations"?*

COACHEE: *Well, I wasn't great in this one, but sometimes—for
example with a difficult customer—I focus on them,
not me, and can be great under pressure.*

In this way the coach is taking each Pessimist and Judge statement
and helping the coachee test it out. *What is the truth here*? Once the
coachee finds the truth, their fears and judgments will no longer have a
hold on them. This means they can move to the next stage: C, for Choice.

Step Three: Choice

What is the purpose of this step?

For the coachee to commit to conscious choices and move toward learning and action.

Why is this important?

Now that you have challenged the assumptions of the coachee's in-the-
box mindset, they can access more possibility and choice. Committing to
action enables them to apply the learning, thereby growing in awareness
and integrating the mindset of the Realist when they need it.

What is critical as a coach?

To ensure conscious choice and commitment: when our coachee com-
mits to an action, they are far more likely to go through with it.

Choice

Step Three follows from Step Two. It is made possible by Step Two, because
in Step Two the coachee has established the truth around the situation.

The coach is effectively asking the coachee, "Given this truth, what
proactive choice do you make?"

This is key because it moves the coachee from reacting to leading. A conscious choice of this kind lies at the heart of resourcefulness.

So how did this work in our example conversation?

The coach simply replayed the truths that had been spoken and asked the coachee to make a choice in applying their learning going forward.

> COACH: *So we know that no single presentation is all or nothing, that you want to improve your impact with the board, and that you can be brilliant under pressure—especially when you focus on the other person, not yourself. How might you handle the next presentation differently?*
>
> COACHEE: *I guess I could consciously focus on them. Maybe ask some questions and engage them first—like I would with a customer. And enjoy the situation. Take the pressure off myself and be the way I would with a customer.*
>
> COACH: *And do you have another presentation coming up to try this?*
>
> COACHEE: *Yes, as it happens, I am presenting to the same group next week. I'll use it as a chance to try my new approach.*

Applying the Be Conversation

Application to other situations

You can apply the Be conversation for many scenarios. For example:

1. Managing our resilience and resourcefulness

This has been the heart of the chapter. The understanding and practice of ETC is core to being resilient and resourceful—by overcoming limiting mindsets, it is possible to coach others to be better able to bounce back from the triggers that life offers and turn them into learning opportunities and create new choices.

2. Stress

In our increasingly fast-paced world, more companies are investing in developing resilience of their workforce and culture. Resilience is the capacity to bounce back, to cultivate a positive outlook, to face and rise above difficulties. Not being resilient leads to a build-up of stress.

The Be conversation is central in supporting others with the stress they face. Stress is primarily a physical response, where the body thinks it's under attack and responds by fight, flight, or freeze. Humans wouldn't have survived without it. It is a very useful response to situations where there is real threat or danger. The body releases hormones and chemicals such as adrenaline, cortisol, and norepinephrine to get ready for action. This causes a number of reactions, such as heart rate speeding up, and the shutting down of certain functions by diverting blood to important muscles.

However, the body can still go into a stress response in situations that don't require it. The Be conversation speaks to this precisely—and addresses how to change mindset in response to these situations that appear to cause stress.

There is good news and bad news. The bad news is that the work environment will continue to have its ups and downs. The good news is that coachees can still choose their response by understanding the way in which they perceive and relate to their experience.

The metaphor of the window at the start of the chapter describes it well—the coachee's perception is the "window" or lens through which they look at their experience. Change the lens, and the experience changes and enables them to access new choices.

3. Confidence

When someone is low in confidence, there is a direct correlation with the self-doubting or critical assumptions from the Judge and Pessimist.

You can coach them by working through the steps of ETC to become aware of and let go of the doubting or critical voice that feeds insecurity and uncertainty (Step One). Then, you can coach them to connect with the Realist by drawing strength from a time when they felt confident or compassionate toward themselves (recent research has shown that self-compassion leads to greater self-esteem).[3] This enables people to tell the truth about those exaggerated critical and self-doubting voices (Step Two). Finally, you can coach them to make conscious choices and apply what they've learned when negative self-talk is triggered (Step Three).

4. Managing emotional outbursts

When a colleague is emotionally flooded, spending more time on the "E" step is helpful. You give them the space to vent and release their emotion in this step first. A useful tip: when someone is emotionally flooded, inviting them to talk and bring more reason into their thinking can help them rebalance. Equally, someone who is rationally flooded will find some balance by connecting with their feelings.

5. Leadership presence

The quality of presence is important for leaders. The opposite of the word *presence* is *absence*. Sometimes when situations get tough, people withdraw or run away (or sometimes we fight). Either way, the conscious self is not present and connected in the moment. They are "away" with their self-talk. By working through ETC, the person can face and be present to their feelings. They can work through the process so that they are still available, connected, and contributing—they are present with a conscious and truth-telling mindset, rather than lost in their limiting mindset.

6. Changing behavior

When someone is trying to change specific, hard-to-change behaviors, the biggest hurdle can be the old mindset. With any new behavior, the person needs to let go of the mindset driving the old behavior and embrace the new mindset that will unlock the new behavior. So, we can use ETC to look at the behavior they want to change and explore the trigger when the old behavior is activated. By looking at the self-talk and challenging it with the mindset of the Realist, they can start to let go of the mindset that drives the old behavior and replace it with the healthy mindset that drives the new behavior. For example, a coachee may want to go to the gym three times per week—the new behavior. The old behavior might be that they come home, put their keys down, and switch on the TV. The mindset driving this might be: "I need to relax. Watching TV helps me relax. If I don't watch TV, I will not get the space I need." Clearly, there are assumptions that are not quite true from the perspective or mindset of the Realist. Exercise is far more effective in relaxation than is watching mind-numbing TV. As they engage their Realist mindset, they can challenge the self-talk in the trigger moment, then engage and embrace the truth that "I actually feel better when exercising—healthier, more fit, and energized." This is the new mindset. They can then experiment with the new behavior, applying this new mindset consciously, until the new behavior is integrated.

7. Prevention of potentially difficult situations

It can be helpful to prepare our coachees for potential triggers around the corner. How? By engaging the Realist and noticing rather than getting hooked by the reactions that arise. For example, a coachee may have an important presentation or meeting that could have trigger points. By spending a few moments preparing and connecting with their Realist in advance, they can save themselves the suffering of going in the box first.

Here is an example.

COACH: *OK. Imagine yourself on the stage. You look down at all the people. What are you feeling?*

COACHEE: *Nervous. Feel tight and my heart is racing.*

COACH: *And what are you telling yourself?*

COACHEE:	*"They won't be interested in what I have to say." "I'll mess it up." "I'm not as good as the previous speaker."*
COACH:	*OK. Take a breath. Is it true the audience won't be interested in what you have to say?*
COACHEE:	*No. Well, actually, as I think about it, my message is really important for them.*
COACH:	*And will you mess it up?*
COACHEE:	*I don't know at this stage. But I know I can deliver this message really well.*
COACH:	*OK—given that you know the message is important and that you can deliver it well, what choice can you make for the moment you step on stage?*
COACHEE:	*I can focus on the message and how important it is. When I do this, I feel confident and excited.*

8. Sleep and recovery

Overactive minds have a direct impact on people's ability to recover and rest. The Be conversation is a powerful tool to help coachees regain a state of relaxation because 1) you consciously give voice to the self-talk and give conscious space to the feelings, and 2) you calm them down through their Realist, leaving them in a much more peaceful state. On a personal level you could try this by experimenting with ETC before going to bed to work through any feelings and self-talk associated with being in the box from the day.

The business impact

Research shows that our inner states contribute directly to our performance. For example, a Harvard study based on 26 teams in seven companies found that positive inner lives have a positive impact on creativity and productivity as well as the perceptions of colleagues. This is reinforced by studies from University of London Professor Frank Bond and others, which show that the emotional agility of the Be conversation can help people alleviate stress, reduce errors, become more innovative, and improve job performance.[4]

Research undertaken by meQuilibrium shows some amazing findings. For example, looking at staff turnover alone, employees with low resilience scores are twice as likely as those with high resilience to quit within the next six months—which clearly has direct impact on the business financials, because there is a significant cost to replacing individuals in organizations. Other equally interesting data in this research shows the impact on well-being and effectiveness: people who are more resilient are less likely to underperform.[5]

Practicing and applying it to yourself

Think about a situation where the Be conversation is going to be useful. Maybe you went in the box, lost your confidence, or found yourself in a situation where you weren't resourceful. See if you can find the moment where your state significantly changed (note, this may require some thought to see where you moved from one state to another).

1. Step One: Emotions (and self-talk)

Take yourself back to the trigger event:

- What is the specific trigger?
- How are you feeling in the moment of trigger?
- What's your body language and physiological responses in the box?
- What is your self-talk? What are your Pessimist and Judge saying?
- If that statement is true, then…?
- What does that mean about you?

In this step, you are becoming aware of your reactions and self-talk in response to the trigger event.

Breathe: Now take a breath or two. Breathe, let go, relax.

2. Step Two: Truth

Now take a moment to imagine a time where you were out of the box. Imagine yourself there now:

- How do you feel?
- Review some self-talk statements, one at a time, and answer: what is the truth about that statement now?
- What is important to you here?

In this step you are connecting with the Realist and challenging the self-talk that keeps you in the old mindset or lens.

Breathe: Now take a breath or two. Breathe, let go, relax.

3. Step Three: Conscious Choices

- What choices come to you now?
- What are your options?
- What can you do differently in this situation or if this situation were to occur again?
- How might you use this tool going forward?
- What action do you commit to?
- What have you learned?

The key in the step is to act on the shift in mindset. By making conscious choices and commitments to action, you are giving yourself the best possible chance of growth and change.

Breathe: Now take a breath or two. Breathe, let go, relax.

Note the importance of the breath: research by Dr. Jose Herrero, in collaboration with Dr. Ashesh Mehta, a renowned neurosurgeon, shows that willfully controlling your breath gives further access and integration to the different parts of the brain. This can lead to greater calmness and emotional control. Deep breathing literally "changes your mind."[6]

Applying it in coaching: other great coaching questions

You can use the questions in the previous section in your coaching. Here are some other ones.

1. Coaching the E stage

- What was the trigger—the exact incident that evoked your reaction (e.g., words that were said verbally or in an email, an action or behavior from someone)? The more factual we can get about the trigger, the easier it is for us to see the interpretation we overlay.

- What is the cost of going in the box—on you, on others, on your work?

- Is this a pattern of reaction to this type of trigger for you?

- What might others see you doing if you are triggered?

- What are the cues that tell you that you are in the box?

- If (add statement) is true, then what does that mean to you or what does that say about you? (This helps to uncover the layers of the self-talk.)

2. Coaching the T stage

- Play back in your coachee's words their Pessimist and Judge statements. Ask for each statement, "Is that really true? What is the truth about that?"

- Be prepared to keep asking, "Is that really true?" Your coachee may need to wrestle with this question.

- What is important to you here?
- What other possible perspectives could be true?

3. Coaching the C stage

Play back the true statements that come from the T stage. Pose these questions:

- Given this, what choice do you want to make?
- How will you respond differently to the situation?
- If you were to get really creative, what other choices do you now have?
- How will you respond differently to similar situations in the future?
- What have you learned about yourself?
- What other types of triggers can you apply your learnings and insights to?
- How will this process benefit you in your leadership and in the achievement of your objectives?

Hints and tips to shift from in the box to out of the box

If the ETC process isn't right, here are some other ways people can become more resourceful.

Physical	
Our feelings occur in our body, so making physical changes can help us change our state.	• Take a break/slow down/count to 10/take a few deep breaths. • Change your physical state/be active (exercise is a great way to change state, but something as simple as physical movement can help).

	• Looks after yourself physically (i.e., diet, exercise, rest), especially during demanding times. We are much more likely to be triggered when we are tired, lethargic, nutritionally imbalanced, overloaded.
Focus Often spending time getting clear on what we want (rather than on our fears) helps us rediscover our perspective.	• Remind yourself of your purpose—what does this situation really need? • Remind yourself of what is really important—what are the values you would like to express here?
People You can only listen to one thing at a time—either to your own self-talk or to other people. Focusing on others can also restore balance.	• Get into other people's shoes—start listening to others; "see" and "hear" them fully. Restate what you hear. Get curious about where they are coming from.
Thoughts This is the most powerful set of tools, as they are changing the root cause (our self-talk).	• Begin to notice your patterns—what are the types of events/situations that put you in the box? What themes do you notice?

Summary

This conversation

- Is great when someone is feeling lousy, unconfident, or unresourceful;

- Is useful to overcome going "in the box" and find someone's best and resourceful self in their leadership when they most need it;

- Involves three key steps:

  ○ Emotions (and self-talk)

    This is about recognizing the lens through which the coachee sees—the lens comprises their self-talk, with corresponding feelings and physiological reactions. Uncovering the self-talk enables us to see what assumptions are within the mindset of being in the box when triggered.

  ○ Truth

    Once we have brought awareness to what is going on when in the box, this step is about the Realist challenging the self-talk. The shift in mindset here is about seeing the truth rather than the assumptions, thereby releasing the coachee from getting stuck in the box.

  ○ Conscious Choice

    The coachee can now apply their shift in mindset to making conscious choices about what they will do now.

Through conscious practice the coachee can reduce the sensitivity to the triggers that often show up in their lives and work.

Chapter **2**

Relate

Understanding and Identifying the Conversation

Introduction

When do we use this conversation?

What a coachee might say

How to recognize the shift

The Relate Conversation

A sample conversation in action

Breaking down the conversation at a high level: the See-Hear-Speak process

Breaking down the conversation in detail: the coaching insights and models

Step One: See

Step Two: Hear

Step Three: Speak

Applying the Relate Conversation

    Application to other situations

    The business impact

    Practicing and applying it to yourself

    Applying it in coaching: other great coaching questions

Summary

Understanding and Identifying the Conversation

Introduction

When someone needs to build trust or connection with others

In chapter 1 we posed this scenario:

> Imagine you lead a sales team. One of your top account executives has been trying to close a deal. Every one of the key decision makers in the customer business is on board except for one finance director. "I've tried everything," fumes your team member, "but he's so small minded. All he thinks about is cost—what can I do?"

How do you respond? How can you coach him to learn from this and find a new way to influence the finance director?

In this chapter we'll explore the answer. And in doing so we'll explore what is possibly the most common coaching conversation.

Consider this story, a radio exchange on the sea at night:

RADIO OPERATOR 1:   *Radio Operator 2, we are heading in your direction and our radar has spotted you.*

	We request you move 15 degrees due north to avoid collision. Please respond, over.
RADIO OPERATOR 2:	*We cannot commit to such an action and request you move your ship, over.*
RADIO OPERATOR 1 (LOUDER):	*We ask you to move 15 degrees due north now, over.*
RADIO OPERATOR 2:	*We repeat, we cannot take such action and once again request you move your ship's heading, over.*
RADIO OPERATOR 1:	*WE DEMAND YOU CHANGE YOUR DIRECTION IMMEDIATELY, OVER.*
RADIO OPERATOR 2:	*This is a lighthouse, your choice. Over and out.*

In this story, we see the first operator getting louder to direct and influence change in the second operator, when in fact simply trying to understand the other person would have revealed the reason why the request was impossible to meet. Then, a workable solution could have been found. How many times have you seen this in the work environment? Often leaders try to direct and influence others by getting louder instead of seeking to understand and find a solution that would benefit all sides.

The Relate conversation is about this situation—and a lot more. It is coaching people to let go of their own assumptions about other people and find a better way of dealing with others through empathy and relationship. *The mindset shifts from "only" my view to empathizing and embracing the views of others.*

By mastering this conversation, you will be able to help others improve their relationship with a manager, become better at giving difficult messages, or become more influential—winning hearts and minds.

Let's take another example that parallels the lighthouse metaphor. A leader was in charge of the strategy for delivering a new product to market. The operations team was trying to explain that the expected delivery time was unrealistic. Instead of listening to the reasons, the leader became more heavy handed, firing off emails to senior leaders that this approach was not going to work given the commitment to the customer. While the relationships became strained, the wider impact was that the operations team delivered a poor-quality product that did not meet the needs of the customer.

This can be common, especially in the high-pressure environments that are often encountered today. Many people don't take the time to stop and listen, to see what the real issue is, nor do they take the time to share their needs clearly enough. The result is more stress and relationship tension.

Through coaching, the leader began to acknowledge and listen to the the operations team, whose members felt like they lacked the resources to meet the timeline. After listening, the leader went on to explain the importance of meeting the requirement—it was a pilot that would significantly impact the bottom line and could deliver a new product line in an ever-competitive market. Now that he and the other teams were able to understand each other, they were able to find a solution that everyone aligned with: to take the risk and invest in some new machinery that would speed up the production process. The impact was a better outcome for all, with relationships still intact. In fact, the relationships were stronger.

Because businesses operate more globally and in a more interconnected way than ever before, the need to influence and work well with others is ever more important. Often there are additional challenges due to differences in culture. There are plenty of instances where our organization is called in to support leaders working across cultures because there is lack of skill in working with difference and diversity. We hear stories of ex-pat leaders pushing their style onto a new culture, judging the differences, and creating antagonizing work environments. This conversation is great for understanding, respecting, and embracing different cultures.

When do we use this conversation?

Obviously Relate topics are all about people—and your coachee's effectiveness at dealing with them. Often you can recognize the need for a

Figure 2-1: Relate topics and challenges

Relate coaching conversation because there are particular individuals or groups that your coachee struggles with, or particular interactions that are going wrong.

Here are some common examples.

What a coachee might say

For the Relate shift, you should listen for the following:

- A lack of empathy. Are they fully able to put themselves in the shoes of other people and experience other people's worlds?

- Assumptions about how others will think. "If I have the difficult conversation, then they will get upset."

- A lack of curiosity about others. Assumptions about what others need or how to treat them.

- Misunderstandings, strong emotional reactions, or frustrations with others expressed out loud. "My manager isn't interested in me," "They are so annoying," or "He doesn't care about my projects."

How to recognize the shift

The shift in Relate is all about empathy. If your coachees can quickly experience other people's worlds and see what really matters to them, they can flex their response accordingly. It will unlock new possibilities with the individual or group they are struggling with, and also open up a much wider range of alternatives to them in their dealing with all individuals.

Look for situations where your coachees are struggling to connect, influence, or engage a person or a group. The chances are that these are "learning moments," which—if you coach with this conversation in mind—can unlock new insight into how to take others with them more broadly in life.

The Relate Conversation

A sample conversation in action

We will first look at the Relate conversation in the context of influencing or taking people with you, as it is so important in today's world. Later, we will show how the Relate conversation applies to many other contexts where we relate to others in the workplace—such as coaching others, having great conversations, and working with conflict.

So let's see the Relate conversation in full. And, as with Be, we'll do this by going back to the case study we introduced both in the introduction and at the beginning of this chapter. How might a great coach help the account executive deal with his finance director client?

....

When the account executive comes in frustrated at the response he is getting from the finance director, the coach says, "That sounds frustrating. What do you need?"

The account executive replies, "I need to find a way of getting the finance director on my side."

The coach agrees to support him with his goal.

Part One ("See")

COACH: *Think back to your last meeting, as if you were there. How do you remember him behaving?*

COACHEE: *He is sitting behind his desk and a pile of papers. He is guarded in answering questions. He keeps challenging the cost.*

COACH: *And how do you respond? What feelings come up? What are you telling yourself?*

COACHEE: *I get frustrated. I start telling myself this guy is just a blocker.*

COACH: *How do you think that impacts your behavior?*

COACHEE: *I lean forward to try to make my case as clear as possible.*

COACH: *OK, now let's look at the situation from his point of view. Imagine yourself in his world. You are looking at an account executive who is leaning forward and trying to make his case as clear as possible. What do you feel? What are you telling yourself?*

COACHEE: (Speaking as the finance director): *I feel intimidated. I close off. I think this guy is really trying to push something.*

COACH: *How then do you respond, still as the finance director?*

COACHEE: *I become closed. Try and get him out as quick as possible. That is what actually happened.*

COACH: *Now imagine yourself as a wise witness looking at the finance director and the account executive. What do you notice? What is your advice?*

COACHEE: *I'm seeing it now. The account executive's frustration is causing him to push harder, which the finance director reacts to by stepping back. The account executive should go slower, stop pushing. He should ask the finance director to say more about what his concerns are.*

Part Two ("Hear")

COACH: *Great. Now using this insight into the finance director's world, how can you let him feel heard?*

COACHEE: *I'll keep playing back his concern. Keep asking if there is anything else.*

COACH: *Anything else you wish to experiment with? What might be your stretch with listening at a deeper level, now that you are open to seeing his world?*

COACHEE: *I might try to listen for the feelings behind the concerns so that I can really understand the concerns at a deeper level, and thereby address these if needed.*

Part Three ("Speak")

COACH: *Obviously you'll not know how you can communicate your pitch differently until you've heard him. But any thoughts at this stage?*

COACHEE: *Of course I'll wait. But as I think about it, I think I can already imagine changing the presentation to speak more clearly to his financial concerns. I really get why that is important to him, and I need to address that in my pitch.*

By using the Relate conversation, the account executive has found a new way of engaging with a critical sales contact. But more than that, the coachee has a way of thinking that will help him find a new way of engaging with anyone he finds challenging.

Breaking down the conversation at a high level: the See-Hear-Speak process

So what just happened here? The Relate coaching conversation is based on a simple metaphor. The one we use is called See-Hear-Speak, or the three monkeys.

Traditionally the three monkeys are often drawn sitting side by side. The one on the left covers his eyes (signifying "see no evil"), the one in the middle covers his ears (signifying "hear no evil") and the one to the right covers his mouth (signifying "speak no evil").

The order of the monkeys provides a route and a pathway for influencing others and taking people with you. When practiced well, this is both extremely simple yet incredibly powerful. The trick is to follow the

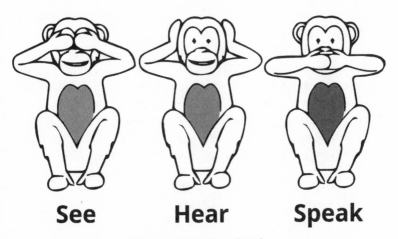

See   **Hear**   **Speak**

Figure 2-2: See Hear Speak

steps in turn and not move on to the next one until its predecessor has been completed.

So, what are the three steps?

Step One: See

The first monkey, or step, is about letting other people know that they are seen. It is about breaking down barriers, building trust, and developing mutual respect. When someone feels "seen," they will speak openly. Any defensiveness or suspicion will disappear. They will feel comfortable talking about the particular issues at that particular time.

In the example conversation, we saw the coach begin coaching the account executive to "see" and enter the world of the finance director.

To truly see and understand the essence of Relate, you need to start with the insight that every human being has a fundamental need to be seen. This means that true empathy is so often the key. True empathy relies on understanding that other people live in worlds very different from our own, and then being able to experience their reality.

Research backs this up. For example, the Center for Creative Leadership analyzed data from more than 6,000 managers from 38 countries. They found that empathy from managers is positively related to job performance.[1]

Ryszard Praszkier, a researcher at University of Warsaw, explains that empathy activates the "mirror neuron" network, and that there is a "synchronization" process between brains and individuals.[2] This is why you might cry at a sad movie—you empathize with a character and your brain has synchronized with one of the characters. As Praszkier notes, when you are mirroring someone else, you both become capable of "seeing and experiencing the world through each other's eyes." This elevates the level of trust and openness, and both parties become comfortable sharing more about what is really on their minds.

Even though it is a natural need of human beings to want to be seen, it is unfortunately not always natural to "see" them. Even with the best of intentions, most people learn rules for dealing with others: "Feedback can be upsetting so do it gently," or, "Always treat people the way you'd want to be treated," and so on. Getting in other people's shoes is often about shattering these myths. As a result, it's about being able to communicate in the most effective way based on the reality of the individual in front of you. Doing this allows the most challenging conversations to happen in a productive way.

Step Two: Hear

The second step is about ensuring the other person feels heard. This is not simply about listening. The coachee may have listened very attentively, but if the other person does not believe the coachee understands, this will have little or no effect. For "hearing" to happen, the other person will need to feel that their input is being listened to and valued by the coachee.

In the example conversation, the coach explicitly asked the account executive (coachee) how they might listen to the finance director in a way that made them feel heard.

Step Three: Speak

The third monkey, or step, is about communicating exactly what the coachee wants in a clear, exact, and nonconfrontational way.

This was the final question the coach asked to help the account executive think about how to get their message across in a way that expresses what's important to all involved, enabling the situation to move forward productively.

The Sequence of Monkeys

This sequence is very easy to say but notoriously difficult to do in practice. It is likely that both you and your coachee, like most people, have a tendency to move to "Speak" far too soon. Either they go straight there and end up in this dynamic: they say what they think, then the other person says what they think; then the coachee says their opinion again (perhaps with a clever argument added), and the other responds again (maybe with a clever riposte); and so on. Or, alternatively, the coachee attempts to listen first but lacks the rigor of waiting until the hurdle has been attained, so the message loses its benefit.

In many situations the coachee may need to go around the loop again. After all, the other person may still not agree with the coachee. But what is important is to keep the cycle repeating. The coachee can notice the response from the other person (see), take time to hear their objections and listen to their perspective (hear), and, potentially, the coachee can explain their proposals in the light of this (speak). The important thing is to keep the cycle alive: see-hear-speak, see-hear-speak, and so on.

Let's dive in to explore each step in more detail.

Breaking down the conversation in detail: the coaching insights and models

Step One: See – Get in the other person's shoes

What is the purpose of this step?

To invite the coachee to see the other person and their world.

Why is this important?

Seeing creates trust, safety, and connection. When our coachee is not seeing another person, it is often because the coachee has their own judgments and reactions that get in the way. Their mindset is clouding true connection. By seeing the world of the other, they are able to let go of their mindset and expand their perspective by embracing the other. This creates empathy.

Critical Models and Insights

1. The Presence Triangle (Fig. 2-3): this model is a structure to help your coachee be fully present and "see" someone. To see others, they

will need to be present in three ways: present to themselves, to the other person, and to the environment they are in.

2. The Presence Triangle exercise (Fig. 2-4) is a great coaching tool to help others do this and shift their mindset. They can start to touch and feel what other people's worlds are like.

The Presence Triangle

To see and be present, there are three dimensions of the coachee's experience for them to be aware of:

- The coachee themselves and what is happening within them
- The other person and what is happening within them
- The environment and what is happening around and between the parties

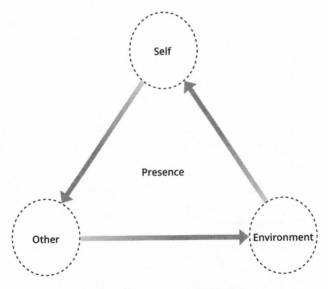

Figure 2-3: The Presence Triangle

These three elements—self, other, and environment—form the Presence Triangle. They enable people to be fully present and remain attuned and empathic. This is critical to truly "seeing."

The Presence Triangle Exercise

Essentially, the reason why relationships fail, or why people fail to sell to or engage an individual, is usually because the two sides don't see one another. This exercise helps to truly understand and empathize with the world of the other person. As a structure for a coaching conversation, it is outstanding. It draws on theories from Gestalt,[3] Neuro-Linguistic Programming,[4] and Cognitive Behavioral Methods.[5]

Have you ever noticed that it is far easier to see both sides of someone else's argument, rather than both sides of an argument you are personally involved in? This is because with someone else's argument, you have an element of distance. Even if you agree with one party's position, you can often see what is driving the other's behavior.

Working through The Presence Triangle exercise helps us with creating distance in *our* own relationships. They are most likely to find insight into how to get through to more challenging individuals if they can move around the Presence Triangle in the following order:

  a. Self: Be present to their experience of the relationship—and be aware if they are in the box about the relationship. Also be aware of the thoughts, assumptions, and feelings they might be holding.

  b. Other: Really empathize with the concerns, feelings, and perspective of the other party—get into their shoes and consider their worldview.

  c. Environment: Look at the wider context, see the dynamics between both the coachee and the person from a distance, and consider the potential of the relationship.

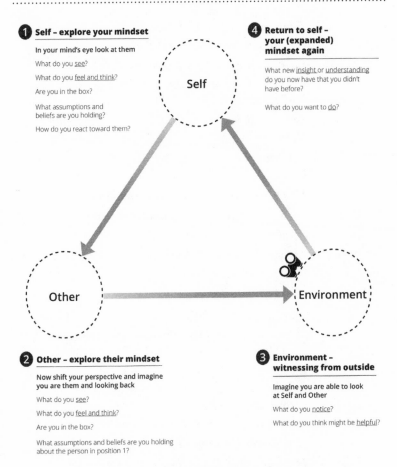

1 Self – explore your mindset

In your mind's eye look at them

What do you <u>see</u>?

What do you <u>feel and think</u>?

Are you in the box?

What assumptions and beliefs are you holding?

How do you react toward them?

4 Return to self – your (expanded) mindset again

What new <u>insight</u> or <u>understanding</u> do you now have that you didn't have before?

What do you want to <u>do</u>?

Self

Other

Environment

2 Other – explore their mindset

Now shift your perspective and imagine you are them and looking back

What do you <u>see</u>?

What do you <u>feel and think</u>?

Are you in the box?

What assumptions and beliefs are you holding about the person in position 1?

3 Environment – witnessing from outside

Imagine you are able to look at Self and Other

What do you <u>notice</u>?

What do you think might be <u>helpful</u>?

Figure 2-4: The Presence Triangle (with steps)

So how is this used in our example conversation?

You may have noticed that the coach worked with this tool. At the beginning, the coach focused on the first corner of the Presence Triangle, coaching the coachee to become aware of his own reaction.

COACH:　*Think back to your last meeting, as if you were there. How do you remember him behaving?*

COACHEE:　*He is sitting behind his desk and a pile of papers. He is guarded in answering questions. He keeps challenging the cost.*

COACH:　*And how do you respond? What feelings come up? What are you telling yourself?*

COACHEE:　*I get frustrated. I start telling myself this guy is just a blocker.*

COACH:　*How do you think that impacts your behavior?*

COACHEE:　*I lean forward to try to make my case as clear as possible.*

Then the coach explicitly asked the account executive to move into the finance director's shoes.

COACH:　*OK, now let's look at the situation from his point of view. Imagine yourself in his world. You are looking at an account executive who is leaning forward and trying to make his case as clear as possible. What do you feel? What are you telling yourself?*

COACHEE:　(Speaking as the finance director in the second corner of the triangle): *I feel intimidated. I close off. I think this guy is really trying to push something.*

COACH:　*How then do you respond, still as the finance director?*

COACHEE:　*I become closed. Try and get him out as quick as possible. That is what actually happened.*

And finally, the coach asked the account executive to use the third corner to explore what was going on more broadly. From this position, the coachee could now draw conclusions.

COACH:　*Now imagine yourself as a wise witness looking at the finance director and the account executive. What do you notice? What is your advice?*

COACHEE: *I'm seeing it now. The account executive's frustration is causing him to push harder, which the finance director reacts to by stepping back. Go slower. Stop pushing. Ask the finance director to say more about what his concerns are.*

Step Two: Hear – Listening with an open heart

What is the purpose of this step?

To help the coachee listen and understand the other person.

Why is this important?

By listening, your coachee can understand what is important, get to the heart of the matter, and take the conversation forward. When the other person feels heard, the other person can also make space for the coachee's perspective. Equally, your coachee will also be changed by the different perspectives they hear.

Critical Models and Insights

Levels of listening: listening can be very deep, from close-minded listening, where the coachee is not listening at all, to open-minded and open-hearted listening, where they deeply empathize and are changed by what they hear.

Levels of Listening

The purpose of Hear is to ensure the other person feels heard. Sometimes this can be rational—it's about listening to the other person's point of view and concerns before building on them. At other times a deeper kind of listening is required. This is especially true for important issues, issues that are difficult, or issues with high levels of emotion attached. We call this listening with an open heart.

So, what does it take from listeners? And how can a coachee deepen their listening?

| RATIONAL LISTENING *Important for practical challenges* | **LISTENING TO SOLVE** Otto Scharmer describes this as listening with a *closed mind*.[6] | You are not paying attention to what the other person is saying, but rather thinking about how you can fix their problem or persuade them to think differently. It is unlikely other people will feel heard if you are listening with a closed mind. *Here, you often use closed or leading questions such as, "Have you thought about XYZ?" or "Did you speak to the customer about reducing the price?"* |
| | **LISTENING TO THE OTHER PERSON** Scharmer describes this as listening with an *open mind*. | Here, you are paying attention to what the other person is saying—not what you are going to say next. You are open to where their ideas might take you. *Key tools here include summarizing, reflecting, open questions, etc.* *"Tell me about your thoughts for reducing costs," or, "What I am hearing is…"* |

EMOTIONAL (HEART) LISTENING	LISTENING FOR FEELINGS	You are listening for and exploring feelings. As a result, the emotional connection with the other person is much deeper.
Critical for emotional or important issues	Scharmer describes this as listening with an *open heart*.	*Key tools include reflecting feelings and asking about feelings, such as, "You sound worried about reducing costs. Tell me more about your concerns."*
		It can at times also be about really opening yourself up to another person's world and being willing to be changed by what you hear.
		"I'm really curious about how we can work together to reduce costs. I am excited by your ideas; let's see how we can get creative together."

How did the coach use this in our example conversation?

After helping the coachee really empathize with the finance director, the coach explicitly asked the coachee to think about how he might better listen.

> COACH: *Great. Now using this insight into the finance director's world, how can you let him feel heard?*
>
> COACHEE: *I'll keep playing back his concern. Keep asking if there is anything else.*

> COACH: *Anything else you wish to experiment with? What might be your stretch with listening at a deeper level, now that you are open to seeing his world?*
>
> COACHEE: *I might try to listen for the feelings behind the concerns so that I can really understand the concerns at a deeper level, and thereby address these if needed.*

With the second question the coach also encouraged the coachee to listen for feelings as well as thoughts.

Step Three: Speak

What is the purpose of this step?

For the coachee to articulate their message in a compelling way.

Why is this important?

Now that your coachee has seen and heard the other person, it is the right time to share what is important to your coachee with the other person, while aligning with the needs they've heard in the Hear stage. Because they have seen and heard with empathy, they have changed and their message is so much more compelling as a result.

Critical Models and Insights

The elevator pitch: A classic tool for sharpening the coachee's message. This asks the coachee to imagine how they would get their message across in a short elevator ride, incorporating the insights from the previous two steps.

The Elevator Pitch

In the Speak stage, when it comes to influencing, the coachee incorporates the previous stages of See and Hear, and ends up communicating

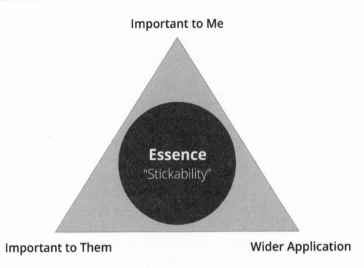

Figure 2-5: Elevator speech

in a powerful way that ensures they have embraced what is important to the other person.

There are many tools for this. In this book we'll use the "elevator pitch" as an example.

Here are the elements.

1. **Important to me.** Why the issue is important to your coachee. This is a chance for your coachee to share their spark and how they personally feel—from their heart. If there is nothing personal in the message, it is likely to lose impact. The coachee can find a simple way of bringing to life the importance of the subject personally—for example, by sharing a story that brings out why this is so important to them.

2. **Important to them.** Why this is so important to the person they are speaking to. The coachee has clearly spent some time

understanding this in the See and Hear steps. This needs to form part of the speech. The coachee can try to build in something that will resonate with the audience in front of them.

3. Wider application. This is about trying to articulate the wider benefits e.g., to the wider organization, to society.

4. The essence. This is traditionally called a "unique selling point." It can, in fact, be broader than this, but it needs to have the element of "stickiness" to it. How will the coachee's message be memorable? The trick here is to find something memorable enough that when it is passed on secondhand, it still works. For example, when Steve Jobs launched the iPod to the world he asked people to imagine having one thousand songs in their pocket. He captured the essence of the idea in a way that is easy to remember and share. The key to communication is often how a third party—talking to someone the coachee has spoken to—understands the message.

For each element, it is important to have proof points (i.e., evidence) where appropriate.

How did the coach cover the Speak part of the conversation in the example conversation?

The coach was careful to finish the conversation by asking the account executive to reflect on how, after the coaching, he might communicate differently.

COACH: *Obviously you'll not know how you can communicate your pitch differently until you've heard him. But any thoughts at this stage?*

COACHEE: *Of course I'll wait. But as I think about it, I think I can already imagine changing the presentation to speak more clearly to his financial concerns. I really get why that is important to him, and I need to address that in my pitch.*

Applying the Relate Conversation

Application to other situations

Situations in which you might apply the Relate conversation include these:

1. Influence

Key situations where a coachee is trying to influence an important plan or project. It is much more powerful to take others with them than to railroad their way through. This has been the focus of the chapter.

2. Conflict

When a coachee is in conflict with someone else or struggling to see another person's point of view, the Relate conversation is powerful. It can take the heat out of the situation and accelerate them toward resolution. You will notice that in conflict, empathy is often the first thing that disappears.

Often, both parties are in the Speak stage during heated conversations or arguments. Using this sequence is a circuit breaker. In conflict, both parties are trying to make their point heard. By seeing and hearing each other, they no longer need to fight to have their positions acknowledged. Once the other is seen and heard, they will be more open to see and hear the coachee, too.

First, the heat can be reduced prior to any conversation by using the Presence Triangle exercise in advance—this will help to give space to the immediate reaction as well as to truly understand and empathize with the point of view of the other person.

Second, the coachee can use the sequence of See-Hear-Speak in these conflicts or heated situations. They can apply the sequence in the moment to guide the flow of the conversation. Seeing is simply about being present and paying attention to themselves, the other person, and the environment. Hearing is simply about listening with heart. The coachee can then move into speak, incorporating the message they have heard before expressing their perspective.

And, of course, there are times when your coachee will need to give a clean and straight message. Sometimes there are situations where the behavior of the other party is not OK. The sequence of See-Hear-Speak remains, but what changes in the model is the Speak step. In this case, the Speak stage is about giving feedback.

A simple framework for feedback is, "When you (state the fact), I thought/noticed (state the impact)." For example, "I can see how work is currently high stress and understand why you have come in late" (See and Hear are covered; now move to Speak). "When you turned up late three times this week, I felt frustrated and found myself questioning your commitment." Once your coachee has shared the message with the other party, you can invite the coachee to move back to See and Hear to listen to the response of the other person before resolving the situation.

When coaching other people, you can also use the Presence Triangle exercise to support others to break free from conflict. The conflict could be a day-to-day one or when working with difference. Either way, the Relate conversation can have a positive impact in growing and moving toward resolution.

3. Coaching

The same See-Hear-Speak sequence can be useful to keep in mind when coaching others. Through seeing, listening, and asking questions, you truly allow the other person to show up and step into their power in guiding their lives. There is no need for you to tell them. The only difference would be that the Speak stage would take the form of offering feedback, direct communication, or sharing what you notice.

4. Globalization, diversity, and inclusion

When working across different cultures and in global work environments, paying attention to, empathizing with, and respecting others using the

See-Hear-Speak framework can form the foundation of great relationships. Many leaders we coach benefit from the power of See-Hear-Speak in these situations. The See step allows the leaders you are coaching to truly empathize with the other person's culture or environment. In the Hear step, they can listen and understand. Finally, in the Speak step, the coachee can share their perspective in a way that embraces their understanding of the environment or culture. Similarly, in diversity and inclusion situations, the Presence Triangle exercise can be great to notice judgments and reactions (sometimes referred to as unconscious bias) so that the coachee can to let go of them, and truly see and appreciate differences.

The business impact

Research on the impact of the Relate shift is extensive. Neuroimaging research confirms that our brains actually respond positively to empathetic bosses.[7] The trust that develops in turn improves performance,[8] and the safety that develops helps to create a spirit of experimentation that is so crucial to creativity[9] and reduction of stress.[10] In fact, relationships and recognition are more important for happiness than salary for employees, which is what this shift is about.[11] And it's needed: a Gallup Poll study of U.S. employees showed that 70 percent of employees are classified as "not engaged" or "actively disengaged" at work, stating further that actively disengaged employees cost the U.S. between $450 billion to $550 billion per year.[12]

At the heart of this conversation is empathy and compassionate leadership, which has significant impact on employee trust, and on organizational outcomes.[13] "Studies have shown how compassionate management leads to improvements in customer service and client outcomes and satisfaction."[14]

In fact, research using measures of physiology and the immune system shows that positive interactions in the workplace reduce employee sick days and increase employee health.[15] This has a huge financial impact.

Daniel Goleman, famous for his work on emotional intelligence, shows that business partners with both self-management and social skills (the Be and Relate conversations) increase profit by 390 percent compared to partners without those strengths. In their research, this amounted to $1,465,000 per year for the business in the study. In contrast, strengths in analytical reasoning skills added just 50 percent more profit.[16]

Goleman also contrasted three domains of leadership: emotional competencies, technical skills, and cognitive abilities. He found that for all jobs, emotional competencies were "twice as prevalent among distinguishing competencies as were technical skills and purely cognitive abilities combined.... The higher a position in an organization, the more EI mattered."[17] He also found that 85 percent of competencies for individuals in leadership positions were in the domain of EI (the Be and Relate conversations are both about development of emotional intelligence).

The Relate conversations also link to giving feedback—when shared with empathy it develops people and grows organizations. Yet 63 percent of senior HR executives said their biggest performance management challenge was managers' inability or unwillingness to have difficult feedback discussions.[18]

So as a coach you'll get deluged with these challenges. *How do I influence person X? How do I have difficult conversation Y? What do I do about person Z?* So much of our effectiveness and happiness is defined by our relationships with others that such challenges come up all the time.

Practicing and applying it to yourself

Using the See-Hear-Speak Framework as a whole

Each step is powerful as is the model of See-Hear-Speak as a whole. Let's look at applying the whole framework to yourself, before applying to yourself step-by-step. With many coaches this will be a useful exercise to do, too. As a whole, this framework can be used when having a tough conversation or a great coaching conversation. The sequence is a good one to practice.

Your Turn: Reflective Exercise
Select an individual you'd like to improve your influence or relationship with.
Look at the See-Hear-Speak model. Where do you feel your current interactions are typically strong?
See – Do you have trust in place so both parties feel seen and can talk openly?
Hear – Do they feel you really listen to and understand their point of view?
Speak – Are you able to articulate your own perspective in a clear and simple way?

Note: You can refer to some tools below if it helps your conversation by offering some practical techniques under See-Hear-Speak.

	Some things you might try to achieve this	**And how will you know if you've achieved it and can move on to the next stage**
See	Try to notice an individual's preferences and ways of speaking/behaving. Wherever possible match them. For example:	The other person talks openly and without defensiveness
	Where (location) are they comfortable?	
	What (if any) small talk relaxes them, or do they prefer to get to the point?	
	Try to "notice" them and build rapport. This can be practical, such as, "Your results last month were fantastic. What have you been doing in your area?" Or it can be more personal or emotional, such as, "You seem hassled. Is there a lot going on?"	

Hear	Active listening means concentrating on what they are saying; use verbal cues, like "Uh huh," "Yes." Also use body language cues, for instance, maintaining eye contact, keeping an open body posture, and nodding to show you understand.	The other person feels heard (this is not the same as you thinking you've understood them)
	Paraphrasing: Repeat back what you have heard in the other person's own words to check understanding. Summarize the main points and needs being communicated.	
	Reflecting: Reflect back the feelings they are demonstrating (e.g., "You seem frustrated with that").	
	Ask open questions, such as, "What do you think about…?"	
Speak	This entails explicitly linking your own ideas to the concerns you have heard in the Hear step.	Your message has been delivered
	Clearly and specifically assert what you want and need, such as, "I want/need/think…because…." Then make your request, "Would you be willing to…?"	
	Once you have delivered your message, be observant about when to move back to See again. You might say, "You look upset with what I have just said."	
	Use the elevator pitch if you wish to share an inspiring message—once you have seen and heard the other, you can use this tool to carve out an inspiring and influential message. This asks you to imagine	

how you would get the message across
in a short elevator ride. For each corner
of the elevator speech triangle, it is worth
thinking about some proof points—more
help can be found later in the chapter.

Practicing it step by step

We will focus this practice on influencing—though each step can be used separately depending on the context or particular application of Relate.

See – Reflective Exercise for Presence Triangle

Think about someone whom you would like to "see" better, whom you wish to take with you. Think about a specific time you have been frustrated or struggling.

- Now imagine yourself interacting with this person in the moment of the frustration or struggle.
  - ○ What do you see? (What behaviors or body language do you see them adopting?)
  - ○ What do you feel?
  - ○ What are you telling yourself?
  - ○ And how then do you notice yourself responding? (What behaviors do you end up adopting?)

Take a moment to let go of this position. Connect to the human being, the other person. What do you value about them? Allow yourself to be open to the fact they may have a point of view before stepping into their mindset.

- Now imagine you are experiencing their world. Visualize yourself as them looking at you in just this kind of situation.

○ What do you see? (In other words, through the other person's eyes, what do your behaviors look like?)

○ What do you feel?

○ What are you telling yourself?

○ And how then do you notice yourself responding? (What behaviors do you end up adopting?)

    (Note: This is the mirror of the step above, to imagine being in the other person's shoes and experiencing the relationship from their perspective.)

- Now imagine yourself apart from the relationship, witnessing the exchange from the environment, watching both parties.

○ What do you notice?

○ What advice would you give yourself?

- Having explored each side of the triangle, what have you learned? What choice do you commit to?

Hear

Thinking of the person, at what level of listening are you operating with them generally?

- How might you deepen your listening? (Refer to the tools)
- What might you experiment with?
- What will you commit to trying?

Speak (elevator pitch)

Now think about your message you want to share to take people with you. Think about how you would get the message across. Ensure it has the four key elements, and that each element has a proof point attached to it.

1. Why is your message important to you?

- What proof point or story could illustrate this?

2. Why is it important to the audience? (If you haven't done so, investigate this question using *See* and *Hear* first—or spend a few minutes to really step into the self of the other person first.)

   • What proof point or story could illustrate this?

3. What is its wider importance? (To the organization? To particular stakeholders? To the wider community? This is a real chance to communicate a sense of wider purpose to the audience.)

   • What proof point or story could illustrate this?

4. What is the essence of your message?

   • What proof point or story could illustrate this?

Applying it in coaching: other great coaching questions

As well as the questions in the previous section, here are some others you can use.

Coaching Questions for See

The Presence Triangle exercise is a great coaching conversation.
Other great questions include these:

(SELF): *Is this familiar? Are there other relationships that feel similar to you?*

(OTHER): *What advice would you give to the person in position 1?*

(ENVIRONMENT):

   • *Looking dispassionately at the relationship, what is the potential?*

   • *What is going on that prevents a good working relationship?*

   • *How might this be resolved?*

Note: It may feel strange, but one extremely powerful tool is to physically move. Identify the three parts of the Presence Triangle from the start, and then move around the different corners as you go through the exercise.

Coaching Questions for Hear

- Where do you find listening harder? Where might it be helpful to improve your listening?

- Which level are you listening to them from at the moment?

- What is your agenda? How might you drop this and simply focus on the person and what they are trying to say?

- What emotions are you hearing in the other? How might you reflect these?

- What emotions are you hearing in yourself?

- How might you know you have been successful? From your experience or from the other's?

Coaching Questions for Speak

The questions in the reflection exercise are excellent and worth using to help your coachee frame their elevator pitch. But other great questions include these:

- After writing your elevator speech, are you OK to practice it with me? What will help?

- Who could you practice with?

- On a scale of one to 10, how confident are you in sharing your speech with others? What will help you to be more confident? How can I support you?

Summary

This conversation

- Is great for when you want to help others improve or enhance relationships;

- Helps others take people with them in a way that values and acknowledges what's important to both;

- Involves three key steps:

  ○ See—valuing and acknowledging the other person and their world

      It is as much a mindset shift as a behavior change—the mindset change will automatically lead to the change in behavior, whether that be a smile, a warm handshake, or simply ensuring the other person is comfortable.

  ○ Hear—valuing what they have to say

      By using active listening, your coachee can build greater trust and understand what is important to the other person. It is a listening that embraces what they say and feel in a way that changes your coachee's own experience.

  ○ Speak—speaking from the heart

      Whether it is speaking in order to take people with us or speaking in order to heal a conflict, the purpose is to speak to increase connection and move forward together.

The sequence can be followed in each conversation or slowed down in order to delve deeper into a particularly important part that is relevant to the situation.

Chapter 3

Inspire

Understanding and Identifying the Conversation

Introduction

When someone can't inspire themselves or others with a clear purpose or direction

In Chapter 1 we posed this scenario:

> *Imagine you are mentoring a high performer. She has been working flat out over the past year and has exceeded all her targets. But she is exhausted and starting to get feedback from others that she is overly driven and not inspirational. She opens up to you, sharing that she's starting to wonder whether it's all worth it, and she needs some support to reignite her inspiration.*

How do you respond? How can you coach her to find a sense of purpose that will inspire her?

In this chapter we'll explore the answer.

This conversation lies at the heart of leading change. It is about the coachee knowing who they are and the difference they want to make. It will inspire them to lean in, take the lead when others are uncertain, and shape an aspirational vision of the future that others want to follow. *The mindset shifts from doing the job to leading with an inspired heart and mind.*

Roger McGough's poem "The Leader" is a light illustration of the irony of leadership without inspiration:

I wanna be the leader

I wanna be the leader

Can I be the leader?

Can I? I can?

Promise? Promise?

Yippee I'm the leader

I'm the leader[1]

Perhaps an even more famous metaphor for the Inspire shift lies in the old story of three men on a building site laying bricks.

The first man was asked, why are you laying bricks? He replied: "This is my job and I have been told that this is what I have to do. I am going to receive a check at the end of the week, and it helps me to pay my bills and feed my children."

This man was generally quite frustrated and resentful, complained a lot about working conditions with his peers, had a high rate of sickness, and did not like his job and going to work.

The second man was asked the same question. He replied: "I am building a wall—we have a goal to deliver this wall by next month. I am focused on success, I will do whatever it takes to deliver, and then I will have a sense of achievement and a nice bonus."

This second man was hard working and determined. He was waiting for some day in the future when he would be fulfilled, which may be when he retires. He will create a new focus once this wall is finished, constantly focusing on the skills needed to attain his next achievement.

The third man was asked the same question. He replied: "I am laying this brick in order to build a cathedral. I have a vision that one day people will look at and appreciate its beauty; it will be a place where people will come together and create a community of like-minded human beings. I am playing my part in creating, architecting, and working together with others toward this center of excellence."

This man was fulfilled and couldn't wait to wake up in the morning. He was an inspiration and role model for others.

The Inspire conversation is about the coachee finding the inspiration and purpose of the third man. It works by first finding the values that really matter to our coachees. This is the true north from which they create their legacy, shape their vision, and express themselves in the world.

The power of creating a vision is so key: it is something that sustains you through ups and downs.

For example, James Dyson had a vision for a vacuum cleaner when he was inspired by the way a sawmill used a cyclone to expel waste. The vision was so strong that it sustained him through 5,127 prototype designs between 1979 and 1984, including many rejections from manufacturing companies.[2] This can be the power of a vision based on what is important to you.

Theodore Hesburgh, former president of the University of Notre Dame, once said, "The very essence of leadership is that you have to have a vision. It's got to be a vision you articulate clearly and forcefully on every occasion."[3] Without vision there is no direction.

John Ryan, president and CEO of the Center for Creative Leadership, writes:

Leadership success always starts with vision. John F. Kennedy famously dreamed of putting a man on the moon. Eleanor Roosevelt envisioned a world of equal opportunity for women and minorities. Wendy Kopp (co-founder of Teach for All) was still a college student when she dreamed of making American

schools better by creating a cadre of young, enthusiastic teachers.
Compelling visions can truly change the world.[4]

It sounds obvious, but in the real world the Inspire shift is surprisingly difficult and often absent. Why is this?

Humans are programmed to succeed according to the expectations of others. We seek to achieve the best exam results, to go to the right school or university, or to get the best job. We want the perfect partner or perfect family. At work we desperately seek to meet the KPIs that are set for us.

This is all normal, and you can get a long way by succeeding in these terms. But all of these are goals that come from others. Most people aren't shaping their own vision. For many of your coachees, there will come a time when they need to reverse this, and the Inspire shift becomes key.

I once coached the CEO of a major consumer goods company in Australia. After two years in charge, he'd guided the business's performance and could confidently meet the profit and growth targets set by the head office. He wasn't sure what to do next.

For him this was the moment when the Inspire shift was particularly relevant. It allowed him to find a way to put his own mark on the organization, which became famous throughout the region as a pioneer in talent development, something he was passionate about.

One final story that may help illustrate the Inspire shift can be found in a video produced by Lead India.[5] In it, a tree has fallen across the road. It is pouring with rain. Motorists honk their horns in frustration. Policemen radio for help and try to control the traffic. Everyone is frustrated. A small boy walks along on the way to school. He looks at the tree and sees it is blocking the road. He tries to lift it. It is clearly ridiculous, and the tree doesn't budge. A few other children try with him and, of course, nothing changes. But a few adults leave their cars and try too. Then a few more. Eventually a large group of people stand by the tree and together they are able to move it.

This is a great story of inspiration. The conventional expectation is to be patient and wait for the authorities to move the tree. This is eminently reasonable, and not one motorist or one policeman thinks to question this. The boy has a different vision. He looks at the tree and thinks, *Why not move it?* This vision is so powerful that it enables others to change their worldview and reality. The tree gets moved without waiting for the authorities to do so.

The Inspire conversation is about the coachee metaphorically finding and moving their tree.

The most important thing to understand about Inspire is that it isn't natural for everyone. Humans are social animals. We are programmed to fit in—and to follow those we admire. We can't help it. This is what makes us a communal species and enables us to achieve so much.

But the danger of wanting each other to fit in is that when someone has a different agenda or their own agenda, it can easily be seen as competing for leadership. And this is not something that has been encouraged over the course of history. Traditionally only leaders shaped direction.

This is why in the popular imagination this shift—and creating a new vision for others to follow—is so heavily associated with leadership.

Of course, in the modern world we no longer want a few clear leaders. We have stopped rewarding compliance, and the only way to deal with the complexity and uncertainty of today's world is for all to lead at times—from our values and with a vision that can inspire. The Inspire shift is becoming more important.

We will look at applications of this conversation to everyday situations at the end of the chapter.

When do we use this conversation?

These are varied but common topics that lead to this shift, including the following:

Figure 3-1: Inspire topics and challenges

All these topics are all about helping others in situations of ambiguity or choice to get clear on where they want to go and to have the courage to lead for it.

What a coachee might say

You can often tell when an Inspire shift is right because you see people speaking about the following:

- Uncertainty. Not being clear on what the right course of action is.

- Other people's expectations. A change is being driven because "The CEO thinks XYZ," or "The role of my team is to meet these KPIs," or even, "My role as a parent is to meet my family's needs."

- Their concerns or anxieties about how others see them. Trying to be all things to all people, rather than having a clear brand and making choices in line with this.

- The need to provide a stronger sense of direction or a clearer vision.
- They may be feeling apathy, heaviness, lost or a lack of motivation.

How to recognize the shift

This shift is all about helping others tap into what is important to them and the difference they want to make. You can recognize the need for the shift when a coachee appears to be responding to a situation without a sense of vision and direction. Often this will be because they focus too much on what they imagine others expect of them. When this is the right shift, you'll sense or hear people beginning to search for a direction. It is especially common in situations of ambiguity, uncertainty, or change. In these situations, the ability to step up and lead is critical.

The Inspire Conversation

A sample conversation in action

As with previous chapters, let's explore how a great coach might coach the marketer in our case study. As described at the beginning of the chapter, because of her driven style she is losing her spark and not engaging others.

When she shares her frustration about "is it all worth it?" the coach asks her if it would help to talk it through and help her rediscover her spark. They agree and the coach begins:

Part One (I – the Important step)

COACH: *OK—think back to when you first started this job. What was it that excited you?*

COACHEE: *I was proud of joining such a well-regarded organization.*

COACH: *And what's important to you about that?*

COACHEE: *I thought I'd be part of making products that improved people's lives.*

COACH: *Anything else?*

COACHEE: *I guess I wanted to work with people I really trusted— and help them succeed too.*

COACH: *So what was important to you was the ability to make products that improve people's lives, to be part of a high-trust team, and to help others succeed. Does that still sound true today?*

COACHEE: *I guess. I think I've just lost sight of it with the workload.*

Part Two (C – the Change step)

COACH: *It sounds as though you do know what you want but you've lost sight of it. This happens to us all from time to time. Are you ready to move on to look at the vision of the difference you'd like to make? Reclaiming your sense of purpose?*

COACHEE: *I think that would be helpful.*

The coach talks a little about how great visions create a tension between current reality and a vision for the change, then asks the coachee to spend a few minutes reflecting on her own vision.

COACH: *So, how did you get on?*

COACHEE: *Really well. My vision is that we really focus on making products customers need. I feel we have become too stuck in incremental improvements. And I realize people leadership is a big part of my vision. I've neglected this. I'd like to be a mentor to others. And to build an amazing team.*

COACH: *This is really important. All of us need to step back from time to time and get clear on the difference*

> *we really want to make. Otherwise the pressure of*
> *targets and everyday life takes over.*

Part Three (E – Experiments)

COACH: *What are your first steps, having reflected on your vision and current reality?*

COACHEE: *The first step is to bring the staff into the vision and to share mine. I will then set up some time with each staff member.*

COACH: *When will you do this?*

COACHEE: *Well, I can set up a staff meeting next week. We can talk about how we work together and also start speaking about how to be more adventurous in the products we launch.*

Breaking the conversation down at high level: the ICE process

So what happened here? The Inspire shift, and the conversation that you've just seen the coach have, is called the "inspire" or the "possibility" conversation. And it has three steps, which you can remember as ICE: I – Important, C – Change, and E – Experiments.

Step 1: Important—Starting with Values

The first step of the process is for the coachee to work out what is important to them. A great way to do this is through values. But by values we don't mean generic values. Concepts like honesty, integrity, teamwork, and so on are clearly "good" things. We learn this through society and its stories. (Teaching values and life lessons has been the role of stories in most societies.) But if everyone has the same list this won't help them stand out.

What helps with Inspire is that each individual typically has two or three core personal values. These are values that are disproportionately strong in them. They shape their personality. People get annoyed when others don't live them. For example, if a coachee's parents made great sacrifices for them, they may value responsibility. And they may get enormously frustrated by people who don't seem to be responsible and whom they find lazy. The good thing about these two or three core values is that they provide a moral compass—and can be used to help determine the kind of vision your coachees want to shape.

It can be helpful to think about these core values in the people we know. For example, Mother Teresa is known for her values of compassion, love, and care. Olympic sprinter Usain Bolt is known for achievement, excellence, and humor. These could be considered as their core personal values that are unique to them. Both of these people might have a value of honesty, but that does not define them. Their core values are central to who they are and what drives them in their lives. (Note: you can see core values of organizations in the same way. Think about the core values that define Ferrari versus Toyota.)

This means the coaching in this part of the conversation is about the coachee getting clear on their own values and how to apply them to their immediate challenge. This is the first step of the Inspire conversation: values.

Step 2: Change—Visualizing the Change

Another core concept that is important in Inspire is framed in positive psychology. If you are cycling down a steep hill and see a pothole, it can be easy to focus on the pothole. You worry about hitting the pothole and the impact it will have. Of course, the more you focus on the pothole the more likely you are to hit it. This is because you move toward the thing you envision. The right thing to do is to focus on cycling around the pothole. The same thing is true in other fields. Great golfers visualize the ball going in the hole. And great actors visualize a delighted audience.

Inspire taps into this element of psychology. By visualizing an aspirational future, the coachee moves toward it. As a coach, you'll be helping others do this in the second step of the inspire conversation, C – Change, visualizing the change.

Step 3: Experiments—Small Steps and Experiments

The final core element in Inspire is the idea of taking small steps. Our brains are designed to reward us when we move toward a goal. It does this by means of the chemical dopamine. Dopamine helps ensure you pursue ambitious goals. If you go back in time and want to hunt a woolly mammoth, it will be a long journey. You will need to undergo a lot of uncertainty and suffering. But the reward is worth it. To help with this, your brain gives you a chemical reward when you take a step toward your goal. This is why vague, ambiguous goals aren't inspiring. To get your reward you need to take positive steps. Your psychology is built to reward this. This is core to the Inspire shift.

In the tree video we mentioned earlier, the boy starts by trying to lift a tree on his own. This is a small step. It achieves very little on the surface. But it creates movement and momentum. Soon two other boys help him. Another small step. It still achieves nothing with the tree, but again inspires another small step. In this way the vision is brought slowly into reality.

So, the final coaching tool in Inspire focuses on the coachee to set up small and simple experiments—the final step of the Inspire conversation: experiments.

So, what have we learned?

- The heart of the Inspire shift is learning how to unlearn our natural tendency to meet others' expectations and instead to shape a vision for ourselves and the difference we want to make.

- This conversation will have three elements to it:
  - I – Important. Tapping into core values
  - C – Change. Visualizing the change
  - E – Experiments. Shaping immediate experiments

Perhaps the best way to see ICE in action is through another example.

> *Imagine you are coaching Brian. Brian has been hired to manage a small restaurant. Morale is low. Service is poor. He has been asked to turn it around.*

Where should he start? This is a classic Inspire challenge—helping a leader shape a vision for change.

So how might this help Brian?

I - Important

You'd suggest that in facing a big challenge Brian could start by thinking what is important to him. It turns out Brian's mother and father made great sacrifices to ensure he got a great education, at times working three jobs at once. This has given Brian a deep value around service and putting himself second to help others succeed. It also frames his view of hospitality—for him "customer first" is not just a slogan, but a deep belief that people come to the restaurant for special occasions, so he should make immense efforts to ensure they have a truly memorable experience. These values are both personal to Brian but will also begin to shape his vision for the restaurant.

C - Change

In the restaurant, Brian quickly needs to assess the challenges. He does this by listening to customers and staff, and he quickly realizes the challenges. But he will not inspire his staff by simply stating the problem, "We need to fix our service culture." Instead, with the help of your coaching, he seeks to flesh out his vision of a "uniquely personalized customer experience" and of a "workplace people don't want to leave."

E - Experiments

In Brian's case he can't get people motivated by the vision alone. It seems too idealistic. His team need small tangible goals. So, he moves on to the E phase and defines some experiments. A simple one he starts with involves setting a goal for each waiter to check in with each table a minimum of three times during the course of the meal. To demonstrate his vision, staff need looking after too. He also changes to a rotating shift schedule to ensure staff have greater visibility of their shifts and hence don't have to find themselves called in to work at little or no notice.

Breaking the conversation down in detail: the coaching insights and models

Step One: I – Important – What is important to you here?

What is the purpose of this step?

To support a coachee to find their core values—the compass through which they can guide their leadership and create their vision.

Why is this important?

Without the Inspire shift, life takes over and priorities are set through day-to-day tasks, expectations, and business demands. By connecting to their core values, the coachee's mindset shifts, and they move away from these day-to-day demands and become inspired, liberating their leadership to create their future.

Critical models and insights

1. Values: identifying your core values by looking at a time where they were alive or identify them using:

2. Letter from the future: a great tool to look from your future to identify the values that are important.

Your Core Values and Letter from the Future

In the toolkit at the end of this chapter we include the "letter from the future" exercise. This is a great way to help others find their core values because it is designed to enable them to express what is important to them, free of

What are core values?

Our core values are the two or three values that are personally most important to us. They usually come from our upbringing.

Typical values include

Honesty	Integrity	Loyalty	Love
Service	Growth	Challenge	Belonging
Recognition	Acceptance	Equality	Individuality
Fun	Freedom	Teamwork	Status
Direction	Independence	Creativity	

today's concerns. If you were to ask your coachee cold what their vision is, you would often find their vision is built around solving today's problems. This is because humans naturally think about what is wrong and how to solve it. By starting in the future and looking back, the exercise should enable the coachee to think more freely about what is important to them.

But of course, this activity may not work for you or your coachee! There are many ways to do this. A central skill is to identify a situation where they feel inspired, from the past or imagined future, and ask, "What is important to you about that?" This question uncovers values.

Here is how the coach used questions to the same effect in our sample conversation.

COACH: *OK—think back to when you first started this job. What was it that excited you?*

COACHEE: *I was proud of joining such a well-regarded organization.*

COACH: *And what's important to you about that?*

COACHEE: *I thought I'd be part of making products that improved people's lives.*

COACH: *Anything else?*

COACHEE: *I guess I wanted to work with people I really trusted—and help them succeed too.*

COACH: *So what was important to you was the ability to make products that improve people's lives, to be part of a high-trust team, and to help others succeed. Does that still sound true today?*

COACHEE: *I guess. I think I've just lost sight of it with the workload.*

What is important is that any Inspire conversation starts with an introspective question about what the other person wants and what is important to them.

Step Two: C – Change – What change do you want to bring about?

What is the purpose of this step?

To help your coachee build a vision from the current reality for themselves, others, and their work, keeping their core values at its heart.

Why is this important?

Creating a vision gives them something real to move toward. And ensuring they face the current reality means that the vision can be motivational and realistic.

Critical Models and Insights

1. Rubber Band: This model helps articulate the current reality and vision on three dimensions in point two.

2. Me-Us-It: These three dimensions are key in any vision. Exploring the change that the coachee needs to make within themselves (Me), in their relationships (Us), and in their work (It). All three are important and work together.

Rubber Band

This second step is about visualizing the change. You may remember the core idea here is that we move toward that which we envision.

One of the most important things about this is to build equally clear images of what they want and of how things are today. Author and management consultant Robert Fritz uses the metaphor of a rubber band to describe this (1989).[6] In the metaphor, the rubber band is stretched between two extremes. At one end is the current reality. The current reality represents an honest, open, and shared version of how things really are. A rich current reality will include not only the business results that need changing, but also the behaviors and attitudes that have contributed to creating the results in the past.

The other end of the rubber band is the vision—the exciting sense of future possibilities. By this we do not mean someone else's well-crafted statement. We mean a vision that is directly connected to your coachee and to their own sense of values and possibility.

If there is a gap between the current reality and the vision, it creates energy. This is the momentum for which we are looking.

Hence, if the current reality and the vision are too close together, the energy is much lower. The rubber band is floppy, with no motivating stretch. And of course, both ends need to be firm. If either is missing, there is no energy. This is often the case where aspirational visions are created without a frank and shared commitment to the current reality.

Equally if they are too far apart the rubber band snaps, as the vision feels unreachable, and no energy is unleashed.

The art of change is in creating the right amount of tension in the rubber band. This means helping others to build their own sense of current reality—and of vision.

Both ends can be challenging but for different reasons. The process of building consensus around current reality can be quite confronting, as each individual needs to look for their part in the problem.

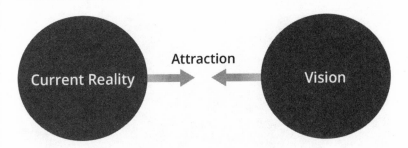

Figure 3-2: The rubber band

For example, a principal began working with an inner-city school. The results were clearly poor, but when he asked the staff about it, he found they tended to rationalize the results ("Our results are pretty much what you'd expect given the kids we work with" was a typical comment). It took him several months of coaching to get to the point where staff were able to say not only that the results could be improved but also that, to do this, they would have to change their own professional practice.

Of course, a current reality on its own does not create the momentum unless coachees find their own inspirational visions for a different future.

Me-Us-It

For a sustainable vision for change, the coachee needs to think about three different aspects:

ME – What is it in your coachee, in their behavior, or in their attitudes or mindsets that will need to change?

US – How will their relationships and interactions with others need to change?

IT – What will need to change in the organization or in the wider world?

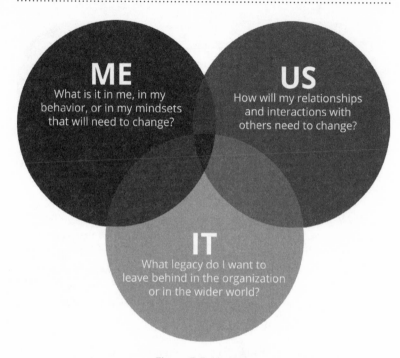

Figure 3-3: Me Us It

Great visions almost always have all three elements in them. This is because the three elements are interlinked, and one will almost always have a massive impact on the other.

Leaving out the Me

The most common mistake is for a coachee to leave out the "Me" part. They talk about what they want to change and not about how they will need to change to get there. There are two big problems with this:

1. Your coachee will lose the biggest lever for change! Ultimately, the only thing they can directly change is what they do. For all leaders changing their own behavior or approach can be one of the most powerful symbols in their armory.

2. If your coachee then communicates this vision with others without talking about how the coachee needs to change personally, this sets the example for other people. Others may look at them and think that if the coachee isn't changing, why should they.

Below is the way an international aid client framed their vision:

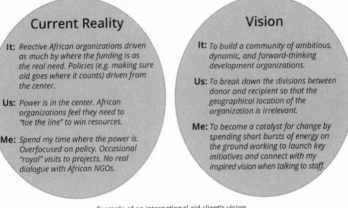

Example of an international aid client's vision

Figure 3-4: A vision eExample

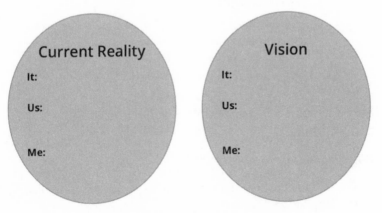

Figure 3-5: Create your own vision

In our sample coaching conversation, the coach uses the rubber band tool directly:

COACH: *It sounds as though you do know what you want but you've lost sight of it. This happens to us all from time to time. Are you ready to move on to look at the vision of the difference you'd like to make? Reclaiming your sense of purpose?*

COACHEE: *I think that would be helpful.*

The coach talks a little about how great visions are like rubber bands. They describe the current reality and vision for the change. The coach then asks the coachee to spend a few minutes reflecting on her own "rubber band."

COACH: *So how did you get on?*

COACHEE: *Really well. My vision is that we really focus on making products customers need. I feel we have become too stuck in incremental improvements. And I realize people leadership is a big part of my vision. I've neglected this. I'd like to be a mentor to others. And to build an amazing team.*

COACH: *This is really important. All of us need to step back from time to time and get clear on the difference we really want to make. Otherwise the pressure of targets and everyday life takes over.*

Step Three: E – Experiments – What small step can you take?

What is the purpose of this step?

To create some tangible and actionable steps that move our coachee toward their vision.

Why is this important?

Rome was not built in a day. Visions are not achieved overnight. Your coachee will need to take small steps, learn, and persevere. Learning and experimentation are key, each time coming back to the values and vision to guide the journey.

Critical Models and Insights

Experimentation and action learning: this is about experimenting with small steps, learning each time and then taking new steps towards the vision.

This means that while all three steps of the Inspire conversation are critical, they have different functions. Values give the client a sense of what is important to them, and vision allows them to visualize the change they want. But without experiments, they create no forward movement.

Experimenting and Action-Learning

As we've discussed, small practical steps create momentum. Achieving these small goals gives you a chemical reward that motivates you to continue.

A good experiment is exciting and feels risky (often this is how we can tell we are learning). If it works, your coachee will have made big strides toward their goal. If it doesn't, they will still learn and end up much clearer about what might work.

The action learning cycle in the diagram shows how experiments form a central part of the learning process. If your coachee is clear about their purpose (the change they want to make) and rigorously keeps experimenting and going around the cycle, the most remarkable changes are possible.

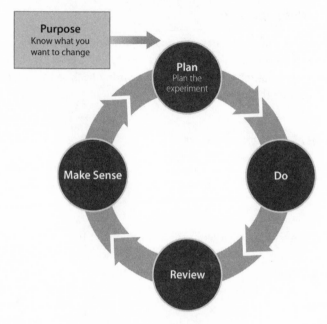

Figure 3-6: Action learning cycle

So how did this work in our sample conversation?

The coach simply asked the coachee to identify practical, time-bounded experiments:

COACH: *What are your first steps, having reflected on your vision and current reality?*

COACHEE: *The first step is to bring the staff into the vision and share mine. I will then set up some time with each staff member.*

COACH: *When will you do this?*

COACHEE: *Well, I can set up a staff meeting next week. We can talk about how we work together and also start speaking about how to be more adventurous in the products we launch.*

Applying the Inspire Conversation

Application to other situations

Other situations in which you might use the Inspire conversation include these:

1. Authentic brand

When a coachee wants to explore their brand, it is helpful to start with values. Who are they and what is important to them? But in step two, rather than shaping a vision for the change they want to lead, instead they could explore a vision for the kind of human being or leader they want to be.

2. Leading teams or leading change

As in Brian's story at the restaurant, shaping and sharing an inspired vision that is important both personally and to the organization's success is critical in gaining buy-in and a sense of shared purpose. It creates the team's identity.

It can sometimes be helpful to work through the ICE steps as a team, devoting time/space to smaller groups or pairs when exploring the future or the values. You could structure a team meeting to explore the steps of ICE:

> I: *Everyone reflects on what is important to them, either through dialogue or perhaps through an activity like writing and sharing letters. Through this we identify, name and share our values that emerge.*

> C: *Together, create a vision on the "us" and "it." How do we relate and what's our vision for how we will relate together (Us)? What do we want to create for our organization, what does success look like, and where are we now (It)?*

> E: *Agree on experiments to make on Me, Us, and It to take the group toward the newly created vision.*

3. Big choices

When someone is at a crossroads in life, values can be the guide that points them toward their true north. So, the steps of ICE are a great tool to find what's important and create the vision that unlocks one's path.

4. Leading in uncertainty

Today, leaders are faced with a huge amount of uncertainty. The Inspire conversation can truly unlock the leadership needed in uncertainty. Start with identifying a situation in which they feel uncertain or held back. Then look at what values are important in that situation for them (Step One). The coaching can then explore what the difference is that they'd like to make and the vision they can see (Step Two). Finally, explore the tangible experiments they could make to start responding differently (Step Three).

5. Midlife crisis

These situations can be very tough. In our experience, this situation comes about when a person has reached certain key goals (such as career success or children leaving home). This a symptom of the current reality that is no longer working and now needs to change. There is a sudden loss of meaning that occurs. "What's it all for?" is a question that arises. It is a critical turning point and opportunity, even though it does not feel that way. Working with the Inspire conversation can help someone reorient toward the next phase in their life. Guided by values (maybe new values that are now more important than before) and letting go of the "old way" that no longer works, a new vision can be created from the current reality that aligns with the next phase of life. It is often the death of the old way and the birth of a new way that creates an invigorated meaning and purpose. The experiments they take will be central in making their vision real.

The Inspire conversation structure is very reliable, but you may have to vary the questions and focus depending on the situation. In all these examples, the sequence stays the same.

The business impact

In a volatile world, where careers are no longer so linear, and leadership is often less about executing on a defined strategy and more about proactively responding to a dynamic environment, Inspire shifts are becoming more important. We can also see some of this in research that shows young people are increasingly seeking meaning in their work. From a business perspective, we need more leaders genuinely connecting to their values.

"Servant leadership," for example, which is characterized by authenticity and values-based leadership, yields more positive and constructive behavior in employees and greater feelings of hope and trust in both the leader and the organization.[7]

And we need more organizations with values-led cultures. Research has shown that:

> *"Values-based leadership, if practiced with a sense of accountability and integrity, can increase productivity and create a culture that is transparent and open.... The values of the leader become the point of reference for their followers to behave in the same manner.... The values of the leader create a culture of how things are done. Some responses indicated the values systems have a profound impact on the organization's effectiveness."[8]*

Richard Barrett, hailed as one of the most profound integrative thinkers of our day, and a Fellow of the Royal Society of Arts (FRSA), has mapped more than 2,000 private- and public-sector institutions during the past 10 years in more than 60 countries, and he stated categorically that "values-driven organizations are the most successful organizations on the planet."[9]

John Zenger and Joseph Folkman's study of 20,000 360-degree feedback surveys of executives found the most influential competency of leaders was inspirational leadership.[10] In their book, *The Extraordinary Leader*, they go on to write, "We have found strong statistically significant relationships between leadership effectiveness and a variety of desirable business outcomes such as profitability, turnover, employee commitment, customer satisfaction, and intention of employees to leave."[11]

Practicing and applying it to yourself

Part One – Important

In the text we referred to the "letter from the future." Let's explore how this tool can contribute to shaping purpose and refining values.

Letter from the Future

Find somewhere you feel relaxed and away from distractions. Pick a specific time in the future that you can relate to but one that is far enough away that you can still dream, imagine, and be open to the many possibilities out there waiting for you. Most people find it easier to pick a particular date that means something to them (e.g., 10 years from now, or a milestone such as retirement, a birthday, or an anniversary). Imagine a future self who has met all of their aspirations. Notice who and what is around.

Now imagine taking yourself forward to that time, as if you are there.

The more you can step into the way things are, the better: what is happening, what is around you, how that feels, what that means to you, who is there with you, who is not, the relationships and experiences you have had, the goals you have accomplished.

Now, still in the future, imagine your answers to the following questions:

1. What has the experience been like until now?
2. What are you remembered for? What kinds of memories and stories will others remember you by?
3. What have you stood for? What would people say about the way you went about your leadership?
4. What is your legacy? What are the biggest changes that you have been able to bring about?

5. How would people describe the culture and relationships you have left behind you?

6. What obstacles and hurdles have you been able to overcome?

Take out a pen and paper. Write yourself a letter.

Reflective exercises

Reread your letter. What clues does it give you as to your core values? What gives you meaning and purpose?

When we are living our values and purpose, we feel on track in life. Reflect on your purpose as it stands today—to what extent do you feel on track in your life?

What insight does this letter give you into what is important to you now and in the future?

Part Two – Change

Have a go at creating your own rubber band. It's a great framework for Step Two in your coaching conversation.

Complete the rubber band for both the vision and the current reality. For each ensure that you are describing the Me, the Us, and the It.

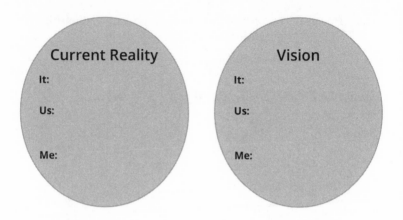

Do not pull any punches in the words you use to do this at either end. The more stark a picture, the more tension you will have in the rubber band.

Once completed, notice how you feel. Where do you feel your attention needs to go first?

Part Three – Experiments

What practical next steps (experiments) can you think of that you can take to bring this vision a step closer?

When will you do them?

How will you know if they are successful?

Applying it in coaching: other great coaching conversations

In addition to the questions above, there are other questions that can be useful in coaching.

A Toolkit of Inspire Coaching Tools and Questions

I – Important

(In reference to the letter from the future)

- What's important to you here?
- Pick an important statement and ask: *What's important to you about that?* This can help to peel away the values.
- If you imagine yourself having completed the role and looking back, what would you like to see?
- What are your hopes?
- What do you want?
- How do these values connect to the values of your organization or business? (This is a powerful question—from our core values, we find that the connection to the organization is much more personal, and therefore, powerful to create alignment within work.)

You can try asking these questions in any conversation where you and the coachee feel Inspire is the gap, and the coachee wants to understand what is important to them.

The letter from the future exercise above is a really helpful tool, and we use it over and over again. Another similar tool is to ask your coachee to imagine what they'd like others to be saying about them at their retirement party, or at their funeral.

C - Change

Obviously, the coachee can reflect and create a Me-Us-It vision and current reality as you've just done. But if you don't have this luxury and want to get there in a conversation, the great questions include these:

- What will be different if you achieve your vision?

- What will it look and feel like if you have achieved it?

- How will other people's experience or relationships change?

- How will you be different?

- How would you describe the current reality? (You can ask this at a Me, Us, and It level)

E - Experiments

- How will you celebrate your success?

- How will you learn from what didn't work so well?

- Which of these do you feel able to commit to making?

- How will you know if you've achieved it?

- What support will you need?

Summary

The Inspire conversation

- Is great to help others get clear on who they want to be and what they want to change;

- Is all about moving away from what others expect and finding a meaningful purpose;

- Involves three steps:

  o I – Important. What is important to you here?
    By thinking about what is important to them, your coachee will be able to unravel core values and a sense of purpose.

○ C - Change. What change do you envision?

    By visualizing their desired future and building the tension with today, the coachee unlocks the natural energy to lead for the vision.

○ E - Experiments. What small steps can you take to bring this about?

    By defining small practical steps, your coachee is committed and motivated to move toward their vision.

This conversation can be explored over weeks—or completed in a few minutes by the water cooler. Both are valid. But the sequence always stays the same. *What is important to you here? What change do you want to bring about? What small step can you take to move this closer?*

Chapter 4

Think

Understanding and Identifying the Conversation

Introduction

When someone needs to find new ideas or creative solutions

In the introduction we posed this scenario:

> Imagine a factory manager comes to you for support. He has
> been challenged to increase efficiency and cut costs. The ideas
> generated so far feel stale. He wants some support to "get out of
> this rut."

How do you respond? How can you coach him around his challenge to think differently and hence to create genuinely breakthrough ideas?

In this chapter we'll explore the answer.

The Think conversation is about coaching to step back, see the big picture, and develop new and different ideas. It is about seeing the situation from a more strategic perspective, about seeking new insights or new perspectives and coming up with a genuinely breakthrough way of thinking.

A metaphor for Think lies in Steven Covey's story, paraphrased here:

> A group of soldiers are cutting their way through the jungle. It is hot, exhausting work and the sergeant is constantly rotating them, so they take turns at being in the front of the line. One soldier—the captain—takes a few minutes to step back from the line and climb a tree. "We are in the wrong jungle!" he shouts, realizing that the troops are heading the wrong way.[1]

The Think mindset shift is about coaching others to get out of their rivers of thinking and climbing the metaphorical tree with curiosity and openness, in order to find new insights and solutions that challenge the way they see the world.

There are many applications that we will cover at the end of the chapter.

The key to coaching Think is to realize that it involves what neuroscience terms stepping outside of "rivers of thinking." In other words, the coachee recognizes that their thinking has become habitual or fixed, and that they need to learn to step outside of this and think differently.

To visualize habitual thinking, imagine yourself getting into your car for a short trip. You hardly need to think about the driving—your body instinctively knows how to start the engine, put it into gear, and so forth. In many cases, if the trip is local, you have probably worked out the best route. You have, over the years, perfected your effectiveness at this task. We call this green thinking. Green thinking is all about mastery, effectiveness, and efficiency. It uses your experience to learn and adopt the most effective way to do something, and in most cases, it is immensely effective. There would be little point, for example, in experimenting by picking the wrong gear or deliberately heading off in the wrong direction. Most people know these things wouldn't help.

But every now and then our coachees will encounter a situation where this green thinking doesn't get them where they need to be. Covey's soldiers are a great example of this. In these situations, it is about replacing green thinking with blue thinking. Blue thinking is about getting curious, taking a step back, challenging all of the rules, looking at things afresh and from different perspectives. Blue thinking takes a bigger perspective and often gets to a very different solution.

But if we knew when to use blue thinking life would be easy.

The difference between good and great breakthrough thinkers is not just their ability to think blue, but their ability to spot the opportunity to do so.

How do you help someone recognize when to think blue? Usually your coachee, or someone around them, will have picked up some signals, but usually they brush them off and get on with their busy days. To know when to think blue, they need to take a moment to notice what they are seeing and feeling. Maybe they feel a level of frustration about a situation. Often, feelings are the unconscious mind's best way to flag us that something is up.

In other situations, they won't be sensing it. In that case, you as a coach need to hold the mirror up to them so they see that they are stuck in a rut and see the opportunity for some blue thinking.

When do we use this conversation?

Common Think topics might be:

Think topics are all about coaching others to break out of "rivers of thinking" and look at problems in a broader, more creative way.

Figure 4-1: Think topics and challenges

What a coachee might say

For Think, we are listening for:

- A lack of understanding of the customer, and an inability to really think through an end-user's lens

- Generalizations or assumptions about how a problem or a situation should be solved

- A lack of creativity; a tendency to show limited thinking in how to solve problems

- A need for insight; wanting to come up with new thinking or new understanding

- Feelings of frustration about how things are currently not working

How to recognize the shift

Think is all about the need to step outside of our current thinking. Look for situations where coachees are struggling to come up with new ideas, or where solutions don't quite seem to land. Often coachees will come to you talking about the issue, or they may even come to you with ideas, but you can see their thinking is closed or habitual. Rather than giving solutions or your own ideas, it may be very powerful to coach with the Think conversation.

The Think Conversation

A sample conversation

So how might a great coach approach the factory manager at the beginning of the chapter? The factory manager starts by saying, "We've been pushing efficiency savings for *18* months now....I'm not sure there is much more to be saved. I need some help to think differently." The coach agrees to explore this with him.

Step One: Looking Up

The coach begins by asking him to list the frustrations in the factory.

> COACH: *What are the things people complain about? Choose one or two frustrations that, if we were to solve them, might unlock efficiency gains.*

> COACHEE: *Well, common frustrations include time wasted due to poor shift handovers and short notice changes from customers.*

> COACH: *Which do you feel might be a good place to look for efficiency gains?*

> COACHEE: *Both aren't new problems, but if I were going to pick one I'd say communication at shift handovers. Often*

> *the outgoing shift is tired and doesn't communicate issues thoroughly enough, causing problems for the incoming shift.*

COACH: *OK, so what is the question that you could ask to get really curious about this?*

COACHEE: *How might we make shift handovers fully effective?*

Step Two: "Looking Out"

The coach goes on to explore how he might gather new data or perspectives.

COACH: *Who might have some interesting perspectives on this?*

COACHEE: *I could talk to team members, to the shift that does this best.*

COACH: *What about outside the business? For example, someone in a factory in a different industry.*

COACHEE: *I have a friend who has just picked up a position running a factory in a business that is renowned for its process efficiency. I could talk to them.*

COACH: *Great. The next step then might be to explore the shift handover issues both through speaking to the best practice shift and your friend.*

The plant manager leaves the discussion with a series of interviews to conduct.

Step Three: Looking Down

A few weeks later your shift manager returns.

COACH: *What did you learn from your inquiry process?*

COACHEE: *Wow, that was really interesting. We haven't ever stopped to just ask. Everyone seems to have some great ideas, but we end up getting frustrated when no one listens. One key thing I have learned is that team members feel less loyalty to people on other shifts than to those on their own shift. This means their handovers are sloppy and extra work is created for the incoming team.*

COACH: *Why do team members feel less loyalty to people on other shifts?*

COACHEE: *Because they don't know them so well.*

COACH: *Why don't they know them so well?*

COACHEE: *Because they never speak to them directly.*

COACH: *Why does that happen?*

COACHEE: *Because there aren't opportunities to get to know people in other shifts.*

Step Four: Looking Forward

COACH: *What might we do about the fact that shift managers don't know people in other shifts?*

COACHEE: *Well, it is tricky as we don't have time to meet each other given the hours people work.*

COACH: *That does sound challenging. People need to know each other and there aren't opportunities. What could be possible here? Perhaps think about how others might solve a similar problem. People in different time zones. Or even your children.*

COACHEE: *That's interesting. My children send each other videos. We could ask team members to make a two-minute video on their phone sharing anything that happened on their shift, and perhaps a personal anecdote. This could be a great way for people to connect with each other.*

COACH: *Great! So, what needs to happen now?*

COACHEE: *We have our quarterly factory manager meeting. I can*
            propose the idea, get some buy-in, and see how we
            can start to experiment together.

Step Five: Looking In

The coach will then check in on progress. Good ideas are never perfect the first time, so the coaching will focus on reflecting on what is and isn't working and improving the plan. Even if the first idea doesn't work, it will be easy to revisit the data and the problem statement and come up with new options.

Breaking the conversation down at high level: the Five Steps of Looking

So what is going on here?

The best way to understand a great Think conversation is that you are effectively coaching your coachee about where to look for new ideas and insight.

So, what do we mean by knowing where to look?

Great strategic or breakthrough thinkers have a constant dissatisfaction with current levels of performance and have a continual curiosity for ways to improve. As James Dyson, the great inventor, says, "Like everyone, we get frustrated by products that don't work properly. As design engineers, we do something about it. We're all about invention and improvement."[2]

To do this they must move their focus. They need to know the detail or the "numbers" and understand the causes of performance. But they also need to look outward and see what is going on in the market—to see the big picture and know where to intervene. In fact, there are five critical places to look and each has a thinking attribute associated with it.

WHERE TO LOOK Attribute	Average Thinking	Breakthrough Thinking
LOOKING UP **Challenging the Status Quo**	Accepts things the way they are. Views current attempts to improve performance as "the best we can do." Experiences a tension between "the day job" and "finding time to think about the future."	Is never happy with current assumptions and actively tries to find new ways of looking at and improving the business. Consciously makes time to get curious, step back, think more broadly, and reflect on the bigger picture.
LOOKING OUT **Inquiring**	Has strong opinions about one or two things that could get better. Under pressure from the task, cannot make time for new learning and exploration.	Looks at every angle for potential improvement, starting to look for live experiments and new angles to try out. Is curious and invests time in understanding more, often seeking out how others might view the same issue.
LOOKING DOWN **Analyzing**	Tries ideas without analyzing their full impact. Often retries new solutions to the same problem.	Gets to the root cause of a problem and understands it from a systemic point of view. Takes time to really think things through.
LOOKING FORWARD **Solving**	Tends to spend too much time seeking the "right" solution rather than moving into action. Holds back from actioning or making change.	Finds a simple solution to a complex problem. Sees a path to action that will move things forward, creates experiments to try out.

LOOKING IN **Persevering**	Abandons and becomes disheartened after an attempt to improve something after one or two failures.	Perseveres with an issue and experiments, continually reviewing, learning, and seeking the right solution. Is not put off when things don't work the first time around.

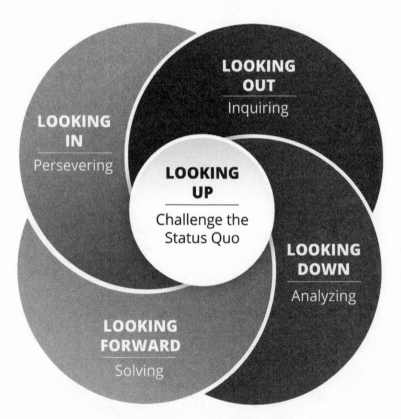

Figure 4-2: Breakthrough Thinking Cycle

Breaking the conversation down in detail: the coaching insights and models

The secret to coaching Think is the Breakthrough Thinking Cycle. The thinking cycle facilitates your coachee to look in each of these directions in the right order. And the order is critical.

First you need to coach to look *up* in order to be able to challenge the status quo.

Then you need to look *out* to seek a breadth of challenge and perspective.

Then you need to look *down* at the detail to find the root cause and develop a hypothesis.

And finally, you need to look *forward* and create the solution before acting on it.

And if the problem isn't fully solved, the cycle is repeated. Critical to this is the "persevering piece," which looks *in*, helping your coachee hold the tension between not losing heart when setbacks occur, while still staying open to feedback and new ideas.

Each different coachee will have natural strengths and weaknesses in how they think their way around this cycle. This means they get stuck or underplay certain parts of it.

The Think conversation has five steps:

1. Looking Up
2. Looking Out
3. Looking Down
4. Looking Forward
5. Looking In

And as a coach you can use your questions so that the coachee can explore each in service to their goal of breakthrough thinking.

Note: At the end of this chapter is a simple questionnaire you can use with your coachee to help them establish where in the cycle they most often get stuck.

Step One: Looking Up – Challenging the Status Quo

What is the purpose of this step?

To challenge the way a coachee is thinking about an issue and move from green thinking to blue and getting curious with the right inquiry question.

Why is this important?

Without recognizing green thinking habits, it is impossible to start looking at a problem more broadly. The shift is from habitual thinking, which has its place, to getting curious and open to challenge the norm.

Critical Models and Insights

- Activity one: From frustrations to blue thinking
- Activity two: Defining the inquiry question

What stops us from looking up?

1. The Reasonableness Trap

Most problems are not new. Things have been tried before and current standards are there for a reason. And the "reasonable" explanations of why this is the case become limiting beliefs.

For example: A marketing manager described a brand whose commercial performance was down. He might have thought:

"We have a limited budget and need to focus on our big brands."

"There has been so much change in our factories that we can't support more innovation at this stage."

"I'm never going to get the same share of voice for my brand that the more senior guys can get with their relationships and power."

2. The Busy Trap

Or perhaps our coachees are so busy solving problems and cutting their way through the jungle that they never find the time to reflect. Maybe they have a sense that something might need to be looked at. But they are so pressurized they don't make the time to really sit and think.

"I never seem to get time to take a broader look and get to the root of this."

How do you start? When you see someone who looks at the world through a fixed or limited perspective (green thinking), how can you support them with Looking Up?

This is the Looking Up phase of the Breakthrough Thinking Cycle, and it is probably the most important one. We recommend two activities.

Activity One: From Frustrations to Blue Thinking

Invite your coachee to take time to reflect on their role or on a challenge they are facing. We are looking at frustration and making observations in order to find the issue. Explore the list of challenges that emerge. Which one might benefit from blue thinking?

Activity Two: Define the Inquiry Question

Once an issue is identified, you can coach to frame it as an inquiry. A good inquiry question is specific enough to define the output you need, but open enough to allow for creativity and new thinking in its solution.

A great way to frame an inquiry question is *"how might we"* or *"how might I."*

For example, *"How might we reduce customer complaints?"*

The customer lens can also help. Consider asking your coachee to think about the inquiry question through the lens of the end user. What need or concern of theirs that is not currently being met will you solve?

Example 1: *For example, Howard Schultz, the former chairman and CEO of Starbucks, noticed that people were struggling to find somewhere that was neither the office nor home to meet, work, and spend time.*

Inquiry question: *How do we create a "third place" where people want to meet, work, and spend time?*

Starbucks coffee shops were designed to be just this: places people could meet colleagues, work on their project, or just hang out. It began with a frustration: the struggle to find the right place to meet.

Why these two activities? Explaining the approach

One of the biggest mistakes around this area is to assume that great thinkers have "flashes of inspiration." In fact, great thinkers are constantly looking to what is around them.

A classic example is the discovery of penicillin.

In 1928 Alexander Fleming was a professor of bacteriology at St Mary's Hospital in London. Returning from holiday, he began sorting through petri dishes on which he'd been growing bacteria. As he did so, he noticed one had mold on it and that no bacteria grew around the mold. He realized there was a possibility the mold might fight bacteria and immediately began testing it on other diseases—and one of the most important discoveries in medicine, penicillin, was born.

The discovery didn't come through a flash of inspiration but through noticing what was happening on dirty petri dishes.

In our experience most people are deluged with data, and if your coachees steps outside of their rivers of thinking they will discover they already have many sources of new ideas. Some tricks to this include the following:

- Notice the data the coachee already has. Often, your coachee will recognize that either they or others have frustrations (like in the Starbucks example—not having somewhere informal to meet) but they don't pay attention them. Because they are so busy, they rely on green thinking and don't spend time on each minor concern. By slowing down, you can invite focus on exploring which of these many issues has a genuine insight behind it.

- Focus on the end user. This is the quickest way to frame a question that will genuinely have your coachee looking out.

- Move from judgment to inquiry. In green thinking we frame our assumptions as judgments. In the airline business there was an assumption that it took 40 minutes to disembark a plane, clean it, and load up a new set of passengers. This assumption was based on years of experience and judgments about what was and wasn't possible. It was only the budget airlines that turned this into an inquiry—"How quickly can we turn a plane around?"—that cut this time to around 30 minutes and saved huge amounts of money.

This means in coaching we are supporting our coachees to take these steps:

- Step back and see their big picture, and notice the frustrations or concerns that they are ignoring.

- Define their inquiry question.

So how did the coach do this in the example conversation?

The coach asked the factory manager to think about areas where people are already frustrated. He then helped the factory manager select one and turn it into an inquiry question. (The example is abbreviated for readability—as a coach you may have to explore many issues before picking the right one for the inquiry question.)

COACH: *What are the things people complain about? Choose one or two frustrations that, if we were to solve them, might unlock efficiency gains.*

COACHEE: *Well, common frustrations include time wasted due to poor shift handovers and short notice changes from customers.*

COACH: *Which do you feel might be a good place to look for efficiency gains?*

COACHEE: *Both aren't new problems, but if I were going to pick one I'd say communication at shift handovers. Often the outgoing shift is tired and doesn't communicate issues thoroughly enough, causing problems for the incoming shift.*

COACH: *OK, so what is the question that you could ask to get really curious about this?*

COACHEE: *How might we make shift handovers fully effective?*

Step Two: Looking Out - Inquisitiveness

What is the purpose of this step?

The second step is looking out. It is about the coachee suspending judgment and seeking data from different perspectives. The core capability is inquisitiveness. The shift is for the coachee to tap into their inquisitiveness and openness.

Why is this important?

So that the coachee takes into account data from different perspectives, often including the customer perspective. It is about opening their minds, another aspect of the shift in mindset to blue thinking.

Critical Models and Insights

Critical to this step is looking externally—especially through the customer lens—as well as internally, and rigorously separating data from judgment.

Inquiring: The Pragmatist's Trap

In our experience, the "inquiring" part of the cycle is often the weakest. Many leaders feel they are busy and think they have a pretty good idea of what is going on, or perhaps of what others think! Spending time getting inquisitive and asking vague, open-ended questions seems a luxury, and many leaders resort to creating solutions based on the data they are already familiar with.

Great leaders avoid this. They know the benefit of curiosity and actively spend time seeking to understand more.

Note: This is shown to be critical to innovation.[3]

Inquisitiveness is a leadership behavior heavily associated with innovation and with strategic thinking. And the more experience a person has in a situation, the more this will depend on taking the judgments they already have and suspending them—and getting curious about what is really true. This is about adopting a true "rookie" mindset.

For example, one small-business leader's judgment about the way they ran their business was "It's too complex." To get the insight, they needed to stop holding their judgment so tightly and get curious. The coach asked questions such as, *What in our business is simple? Where is it complex? How do customers find it? How do our employees find it?* And so on.

Source of data

Once the coachee is curious, they unlock two sources of data:

INTERNAL DATA: What do we already know about the situation? Curiosity enables us to interrogate the data and look at the experience we already have in a different way.

EXTERNAL DATA: Who else has information or ideas that might bring in different perspectives? Who might we talk to?

The focus in the coaching here is to see the true richness of the data that is available to them.

Separating Data from Judgment

In the Inquiry phase it is essential for the coachee to separate data (i.e., what they actually learned) from judgment and interpretation (i.e., the conclusions they drew from it). Data is usually

Something they heard. A quote.

Something they read. Again, a tangible quote.

Something they saw. They may have seen someone behaving in a certain way.

Most people will blur data and judgment into conclusions like "Customers didn't like the idea" or "Research doesn't support this." These are generalities and laced with judgment. On hearing this, we can ask the coachee to identify the real data (such as a specific customer quote or research reference).

So how did the coach do this in the example conversation?

In our example conversation, the coach helped the coachee identify two new sources of data.

COACH: *Who might have some interesting perspectives on this?*

COACHEE: *I could talk to team members, to the shift that does this best.*

COACH: *What about outside the business? For example, someone in a factory in a different industry.*

COACHEE: *I have a friend who has just picked up a position running a factory in a business that is renowned for its process efficiency. I could talk to them.*

COACH: *Great. The next step then might be to explore the shift handover issues both through speaking to the best practice shift and your friend.*

Step Three: Looking Down - Analysis

What is the purpose of this step?

The third step is about the coachee taking the time to make sense of the data and dig down to accept find its root cause.

Why is this important?

It is about getting to the heart of the information. What does this information mean? What conclusion can your coachee draw?

Critical Models and Insights

Why, why, why: a tool to get to the heart of the issue.

> **Analysis: The Solution Trap**
>
> Many leaders find it easy to jump from data to solution. They discover something (e.g., "My brand's budget has been decreased") and seek a solution (e.g., "influencing others to increase the budget"), and in this way they bypass true analysis. They are seduced by the search for a solution too soon. Great leaders back their intellect and know that if they suspend their tendency to jump to a solution and spend time thinking, then nine times out of 10 they will come up with a better answer.

There are many analysis tools around, and it's beyond the scope of this book to explain them. If your coachee has taken a step back and challenged their thinking, and they're curious and seeking different data while reflecting on the root cause behind this data, they are probably doing well anyway.

A simple tool you may find useful in this process is why, why, why.

Why, why, why

This is a simple tool. You take one of the factors that are contributing to the data and ask why this is happening. You then take the answer to this question and again ask why. You repeat a third time using the answer to the second why. For example, a marketing manager trying to understand the decrease in the budget for his brand might use it in the following way.

> QN1: *Why has the budget for your brand been decreased?*
>
> ANS: *Because the business is prioritizing three or four big brands.*
>
> QN2: *Why is the business prioritizing three or four big brands?*
>
> ANS: *Because it can see how critical they are to the P & L. It can't see how important my brand is.*
>
> QN3: *Why can it see how critical the big three or four brands are but not see how important your brand is?*
>
> ANS: *Because our short-term profit plans are better understood than our medium-term growth plans (which my brand would be more core to).*

So how did the coach do this in the example conversation?

The coach also used the why, why, why technique.

> COACH: *What did you learn from your inquiry process?*
>
> COACHEE: *Wow, that was really interesting. We haven't ever stopped to just ask. Everyone seems to have some*

great ideas, but we end up getting frustrated when no one listens. One key thing I have learned is that team members feel less loyalty to people on other shifts than to those on their own shift. This means their handovers are sloppy and extra work is created for the incoming team.

COACH: *Why do team members feel less loyalty to people on other shifts?*

COACHEE: *Because they don't know them so well.*

COACH: *Why don't they know them so well?*

COACHEE: *Because they never speak to them directly.*

COACH: *Why does that happen?*

COACHEE: *Because there aren't opportunities to get to know people in other shifts.*

Step Four: Looking Forward - Solving

What is the purpose of this step?

This step is about the coachee ideating—coming up with a great idea and a plan to execute it. It moves through insight and action.

Why is this important?

In this step, the coachee can

- Come up with their idea and plan
- Turn it into a simple, "fail fast" experiment

Critical Models and Insights

The critical models are simple tips to get the idea juices flowing:

Focus: Start with clear criteria

Flow of ideas: Avoid perfectionism, and get ideas down straight away

Fuse: This tool allows you to fuse thinking with different perspectives in order to generate new ideas

Get stuck and stay stuck: We'll also explore how as a coach you can help by encouraging your coachee to not know the answer; when they marinate on the problem, this allows their unconscious mind to do its work.

Solving: The Perfection Trap

Another common trap at this phase in the cycle is procrastination. Some leaders get stuck at the "solving" part of the cycle as their perfectionism kicks in and they let the many failings and inadequacies of their preferred solution dominate. As a result, they hold back from having the courage to try something different and to bring new ideas to life.

Focus

Contrary to popular belief, brainstorming works less well when "all ideas are considered equally good."

For example, in an experiment by psychology professors at Purdue University, they gave some groups of students classic brainstorming instructions ("No idea is a bad idea") and other groups more critical ones ("We want good practical ideas. Let's try to avoid stupid or silly ones"). At the end of the exercise the critical group came up with the better ideas.[4]

So, prior to brainstorming, it is worth defining the criteria for your solution: not too tight but clear enough to weed out ideas that won't help at all.

A great format for this is, "an x that does y." For example, if we are designing an alternative to a vase, we would say, **a** *way of giving flowers water* **that** *displays them attractively.*

How can you use this as a coach?

Help your coachee define their outcome using "an x that does y" before they start thinking of ideas.

Flow of Ideas

Another interesting myth is that solutioneering is about finding the killer idea. In fact, Vera John-Steiner, a psychologist who studied historically great creators such as Marie Curie and Leo Tolstoy, found that they didn't start with a great idea. They started by sketching or exploring ideas. And they put their initial thoughts quickly down on paper, even when they were only partially formed.[5] It is only by getting things down, wrestling with them, and adapting them that an idea develops.

It is this concept of consciously starting to allow thinking to flow and evolve—rather than waiting for a great solution—that creates great solutions.

How can you use this as a coach?

Invite your coachee to put down their initial thoughts quickly. Remind them that it is more important to capture thoughts than to capture great thoughts the first time. The coachee could also do this as a team, a kind of lightning brainstorming.

Fuse

Here is an interesting insight. If you ask people to invent a story containing three related words such as *brush, teeth,* and *shine,* their output is much less creative than people asked to create a story with unrelated works like *cloud, hit,* and *apples.*

This is also helpful to us. It means that you can consciously use techniques as a coach to stretch other people's thinking.

Here are two you can try.

Fuse Tool 1: Opposites or Extremes

Step One: Create some initial ideas. Ask your coachee to pick one.

Step Two: Ask them to think of the opposites of the idea or take it to its absolute extremes.

> *For example:*

> - *IDEA: "Create a customer portal to make sharing knowledge easy."*

> - *OPPOSITE: "Make it hard for customers to access and share knowledge."*

> - *EXTREME: "Share all our thinking and IP with all our customers."*

Step Three: Ask what new thoughts, options, or perspectives are then provoked.

> - *OPPOSITE provokes: "Only those who are really interested would opt-in."*
>   *"We could then really individualize what's most relevant /useful, etc."*

> - *EXTREME provokes: "Customers could then help to refine and develop our thinking."*
>   *"We'd then create a dynamic community using the wisdom of the crowd, etc."*

Step Four: Ask how these new thoughts or perspectives may help find a different solution.

Fuse Tool 2: Different Perspectives

Ask your coachee to think about how other people or organizations might approach the same problem, such as:

- *Toyota*
- *Apple*
- *Louis Vuitton*
- *A 7-year-old child*
- *A professional sports team*

(Note: These are example perspectives only; you can adapt the list depending on your problem.)

This is a powerful tool when you truly step into these other perspectives—you can use the Presence Triangle Exercise described in chapter 2 to help to step into the shoes of these different perspectives.

Get stuck and stay stuck

What a strange rule. But there is some psychology here too. In fact, when people are working hard on a problem and get stumped, then they are left with something called "failure indices."[6] These bookmarks of the subconscious keep them attuned to potential solutions. They start unconsciously looking for ideas. This is why, if your coachee gets stuck on a problem and leaves it for a few days, often the solution comes to them unprompted from somewhere else.

You can tap into this by encouraging your coachees to get stuck. It's a natural part of solutioning. Rather than the coachee forcing themselves to come up with the answer in a meeting, encourage them to leave the conversation incomplete—ideally stuck around some point. You will be surprised how often your coachee will come back with a really interesting solution.

So how did the coach do this in the example situation?

The coach used a simple version of the fuse tool, different perspectives, by asking the plant manager how his children communicate.

COACH: *What might we do about the fact that shift managers don't know people in other shifts?*

COACHEE: *Well, it is tricky as we don't have time to meet each other given the hours people work.*

COACH: *That does sounds challenging. People need to know each other and there aren't opportunities. What could be possible here? Perhaps think about how others might solve a similar problem. People in different time zones. Or even your children.*

COACHEE: *That's interesting. My children send each other videos. We could ask team members to make a two-minute video on their phone, sharing anything that happened on their shift, and perhaps a personal anecdote. This could be a great way for people to connect with each other.*

COACH: *Great! So, what needs to happen now?*

COACHEE: *We have our quarterly factory manager meeting. I can propose the idea, get some buy-in, and see how we can start to experiment together.*

Step Five: Looking In - Persevering

What is the purpose of this step?

For the coachee to test, learn, and improve, as they implement their solution.

Why is it important?

This is about the coachee staying curious and learning from their failures as they build a sustainable solution that solves the challenge.

Persevering: The Achievement Trap

While architecting a plan is no easy task, this is often not where coachees fall short. If their goal is really stretching and the ambition is high enough, then the chances are that the first time your coachees try to change things, they will (either partially or wholly) fail. Many coachees react to this by changing direction or watering down their ambition. They are used to achieving and are worried about how failure will be seen.

Through coaching they can rise above this by realizing that big improvements are a learning process and that the trick is to keep the high expectations—and to keep iterating their plan until it begins to pay off.

The final part of the Breakthrough Thinking Cycle is, of course, implementation. And we have deliberately labelled this Persevere. This is because true breakthrough thinking rarely works the first time. Effective breakthrough thinkers need to be able to stay resilient and creative as they iterate their way to making their solution land, constantly reviewing and learning so that they are refining their breakthrough thinking.

As coaches, we need to notice when our coachee has gone back into judgment and lost track of their goal, holding up the mirror so that they can learn from the failures and gain strength from the successes. The action learning cycle introduced in the Inspire Chapter could be useful here. This step is about keeping their blue thinking going during the period of perseverance—and remembering to see failure as an essential part of the Breakthrough Thinking process.

Applying the Think Conversation

Application to other situations

Other Think conversations include these:

1. Ideation or innovation

This has been the essence of the chapter. There are different applications using different parts of the cycle. Some people will come to you for help with ideation. Others will be stuck in a certain way of thinking (green thinking) and need a coach to help them look up. Others still will lack the in-depth immersion in what their customers really experience. Encouraging them to gather this data will stimulate new thinking in its own right.

2. Customer insight

By coaching Think you will naturally help your coachees focus on and get curious about the customer. To do this, the inquiry question they set in the Looking Up step needs to be defined through a customer lens, e.g., *What do customers want from…, How can we improve x experience for customers, etc.* In the Looking Out step, the coachee can immerse themselves into the worlds of their customers—truly listening to their needs and perspectives.

3. Strategic thinking

This is a buzzword in business and often not very well understood. Think about the well-known strategy game of chess. Our view is that strategic thinking is the ability to see more broadly, see a few steps ahead, look at the impacts of the choices, and make decisions now that will positively impact our future. The cycle can be used to do just that. The coachee can frame the strategic question, get curious by inquiring (what information is out there), analyzing the data (exploring the choices and their impact), and solving (making decisions) for the future.

4. Challenging the way things are done

Yes, it is the same process and same mindset! Think is the perfect way for your coachee to question themselves in Looking Up and creating new ways to think about old problems.

The Breakthrough Thinking Cycle should be your guide as a coach when a coachee is seeking to work with this shift, but not everyone will need every stage of the cycle. So, feel free to vary which parts of the cycle you use—pull on the tools your coachee most needs—but remember, the heart of the Think conversation lies in the coachee letting go of their green thinking and becoming fully inquisitive. This pattern applies to the cycle as a whole—or to smaller parts of it.

For example, when ideating, you are encouraging your coachees to think outside their normal, green solutions. When analyzing the three "whys," you are challenging the coachee to get curious about the reasons they haven't yet realized. When persevering, blue thinking can support the coachee to learn fast.

As a coach, the mindset shift to step outside their green assumptions lies at the core of Think coaching.

The business impact

This conversation almost needs no justification, as clearly many businesses are built on great customer innovation. To give an illustration of its importance, PwC (PricewaterhouseCoopers) interviewed more than 1,700 board-level executives and found that the rate of growth of the leading innovators will increase to almost double the global average, and over three times higher than the least innovative companies, translating to revenues of over $500 million.[7]

In our ever-changing world, the mindset shift in Think is ever so business critical and key to unlocking the human potential for creativity, change, and innovation.

Practicing and applying it to yourself

Think about a situation where you will benefit from some breakthrough thinking.

Step One: Looking Up

Activity 1: From Frustration to Blue Thinking

1. Look at the challenge you want to solve. What feelings do you notice? What are you frustrated or concerned about? What do you see other people frustrated or concerned about?

2. Can you see an issue that could benefit from different or more strategic thinking?

3. What is the issue you think blue thinking might most help with?

Activity 2: Define the Inquiry Question

1. Frame this issue as an inquiry question: *How might we...*

Looking Out

1. How can you access your blue thinking capacity? When have you recently been really open and curious, and how can you tap into that? What was that like? How did you feel?

2. Where are some sources of data or information where you can find out other perspectives?

3. What questions might you ask?

4. How will you capture the data?

5. What data or experience do you have that you might look at differently? (Now seek out the data before going to the next step.)

Looking Down

1. What are some of the themes from the data in your inquiry?

2. What have you learned? What has stood out for you that is new?

3. Take one of the themes and ask, why, why, why?

Looking Forward

1. Experiment with each of the tools we've covered to see what they generate.

2. What are some emerging solutions?

3. What feels right to experiment with?

4. What needs to happen now?
   (Now do your experiments before going to the next step.)

Looking In

1. What's working well? What could be even better?

2. What are you learning? What improvements can be made?

3. What can you celebrate that is working well?

Applying it in coaching: other great coaching questions

Looking Up

1. What frustrations do you have with this problem today?

2. Who are your customers? How do they experience the service?

3. What needs in your customers are not being fully met?

4. How could you frame an inquiry question that captures this?

Looking Out

1. If you were to think really outside the box, who else could you ask? Think about other stakeholders within the business and people outside the business.

2. What about research and papers online to look for data that is already out there?

3. Who else might have experience or a different perspective? How might you approach them?

4. What questions might you ask?

5. How can you immerse yourselves in their world and experience their perspective?

6. (When capturing data) What did you hear? What did they actually say? (or other questions to help them separate data from generality).

Looking Down

1. When you look at the data, what patterns do you see?

2. What are some conflicting pieces of data?

3. Let's capture the data on a white board and understand or analyze what is being said.

Looking Forward

1. If you were going to be daring, what solution(s) become possible?

2. Who do you need to get buy-in from so that you can successfully experiment?

3. How might you communicate your problem, inquiry, and solution to others?

Looking In

1. How might you stretch your next experiment?

2. How might we use the Breakthrough Thinking Cycle with one of your failures?

3. What are the judgments in the failures that you can get curious about instead?

4. How might you celebrate your success with the team?

The Think diagnostic questionnaire

You can use this questionnaire to help identify strengths and development areas for each of the Think steps.

How to complete the questionnaire:

For each question give yourself a score between 1 and 5 in the appropriate box.

5 – If you consider this an area of outstanding strength

1 – If this stands out as an area that is critical for you to improve in

Attributes	Breakthrough Thinking	My Capability in this Area	The extent to which I feel I prioritize and use this capability
LOOKING UP **Challenging the Status Quo**	Is never happy with current assumptions, and actively tries to find new ways of looking at and improving the business. Consciously makes time to step back, think more broadly, and reflect on the bigger picture.		

LOOKING OUT **Inquiring**	Looks at every angle for potential improvement; starting to look for live experiments and new angles to try out. Is curious and invests time in understanding more, often seeking out how others might view the same issue.		
LOOKING DOWN **Analyzing**	Gets to the root cause of a problem and understands it from a systemic point of view. Takes time to really think things through.		
LOOKING FORWARD **Solving**	Finds a simple solution to a complex problem. Sees a path to action that will move things forward and has the courage to act on ideas; creates experiments to try out.		
LOOKING IN **Persevering**	Perseveres with an issue and experiments, continually reviewing and seeking the right solution. Is not put off when things don't work the first time around.		

Summary

The Think conversation lies at the heart of solving problems, thinking differently, and coming up with new ideas or creative solutions.

It explicitly seeks to broaden perspectives and to help people look beyond their current assumptions.

It is all about inspiring people to challenge the way they see the world, to stop worrying about being right, to get curious, and to look at the problem more broadly to come up with innovative and different solutions

It is about recognizing rivers of thinking, consciously challenging themselves to be comfortable in not knowing the answer.

The Think conversation involves five steps.

1. Looking up: challenging the status quo

Here your coachee is scanning their challenge, looking at the issues and the existing assumptions that they see being made. They are noticing their green thinking and then being challenged to define an inquiry question and get curious.

2. Looking out: inquiry

This is about the coachee suspending judgments and really going out to experience other people's worlds. What is the customer experience really like? What do the stakeholders they usually ignore think? This stage is all about gathering data.

3. Looking down: analysis

Instead of jumping to conclusions, the coachee deeply inquires into the root cause behind the data.

4. Looking forward: planning and ideation

The coachee moves to idea and action. The coaching challenges the coachee to come up with different ideas and to suspend their normal thinking long enough to unlock creativity.

5. Looking In: persevering

The coachee fails fast, adapts, and keeps going.

The Think conversation can be used explicitly to develop other people's thinking. For example, if someone comes to you and wants to become a better strategic thinker or more creative, you can share these steps. But normally it is used in day-to-day conversations to help others think about the challenges of their day-to-day role in a new and different way.

PART TWO

Organizations
Have Mindsets Too

Chapter 5

Transforming
Your Organization

B Y NOW YOU'LL HAVE RECOGNIZED that each of the four coaching conversations come up all over the place. Not only that, but you will hopefully recognize that every individual needs each of the four of them from time to time. This is natural and healthy! All human beings have the following:

- Situations in which they are "in the box" (conversation one: Be)

- People they find more challenging (conversation two: Relate)

- Times that they aren't quite clear about what to do and hold back (conversation three: Inspire)

- Problems for which they can't see the optimum solution (conversation four: Think)

Mindsets are like that. Each of the four shifts we have described is an ongoing struggle. A coachee will never master them fully—but the more adept a coachee gets with the tools, the less time it will take for them to notice the challenge and make a change.

But in this chapter, we want to build on this idea by explaining that organizations have mindsets too, which means you can use some of the tools in this book to solve business problems.

What do we mean by this?

Let's take a couple of examples.

In the introduction we gave the example of BlackBerry. When the iPhone was introduced, BlackBerry was the dominant player. And it took four years for iPhone sales to overtake BlackBerry. BlackBerry had four whole years to respond. Why didn't they? They were stuck in rivers of thinking. They failed to see that touch screens would replace their famous keyboards, for example. BlackBerry's leadership needed a Think shift to challenge the way they were thinking and to respond differently to the market.

Take another example.

A bank we worked with had a highly tuned sales culture. But it had overemphasized this and didn't value serving existing customers. Pressurized branch managers started viewing elderly or complex customers as a nuisance. Soon they were losing customers. Customers were experiencing an organization that valued the sale, not helping them with their problems. The bank needed a Relate shift to get into the shoes of customers and really empathize with their experience.

In each of these cases we find that mindsets run across cultures. The culture of one organization might seek to avoid failure, or another may have strong judgments about a particular group (for example, a country office might think the head office doesn't listen; or a manufacturing site might think that sales are always overpromising). From a sociological point of view, this is not surprising. We are social animals. It is very natural for us to create shared meaning and common rules or beliefs. This is, after all, what makes societies work. But sometimes those beliefs are no longer helpful.

Here's a metaphorical story.

A group of gorillas lived in a cage. A cruel zookeeper hung a
bunch of bananas in the middle and whenever a gorilla reached
for them, the zookeeper doused the whole group in icy water.
Soon the gorillas learned not to reach for the bananas. Moreover,
whenever a member of the group moved toward the bananas, the
other gorillas growled at them because they knew that if any one
gorilla touched a banana, they would all experience the icy water.
Many years passed, and the original gorillas died. But the group
had learned, and the behavior passed between generations. Any
baby gorilla that reached for the bananas was growled at. So, they
stopped doing it, and as they grew up, they learned to growl at
others to teach them the same lesson. After a while there was no
longer any need for the icy water. The gorillas had created a belief
system that protected their culture from getting sprayed.

Later still, a kind zookeeper replaced the cruel one. He had
never heard of the icy water and would never dream of using it. He
also hung bananas up every day and was surprised that none of
the gorillas would eat them.

As this story illustrates, mindsets that were helpful once are often
no longer helpful. This is also true for the bank and for BlackBerry in
our examples above.

And it is almost certainly true in your organization. There will
almost certainly be a Be, a Relate, an Inspire, or a Think shift that will
unlock a new level of performance.

Here are some examples.

Be

A finance department heard that the business was planning on restruc-
turing them to separate out the transactional work and focus in on
its value to advise and provide data to the business. There was great

resistance to this. Worried about job losses and feeling exposed in the new role, team members raised constant objections.

This is a classic Be challenge. The finance department is in the box and not responding resourcefully to the change.

Relate

In the bank example, branches had lost a sense of empathy for their customers. They had become focused on sales and driving the numbers, and they failed to be truly responsive or considerate of the needs of their customers.

This is a classic Relate challenge—where one group of people has lost empathy for another.

Inspire

A large finance business was naturally risk averse but chose to expand globally. Many of its acquisitions had lower standards of ethics, and soon the business was plagued with scandals. Its bureaucratic leadership culture was used to following rules and didn't intervene. Its people felt a loss of direction and purpose.

This is an Inspire challenge. Leaders need to tap into their own values and have the courage to provide direction when it is lacking. On an organizational level, they need to return to the values that drive their business and create a vision that sets a direction based on these values.

Think

A food manufacturer was under increasing pressure to respond to the health-and-wellness agenda. They responded quickly by launching a breakfast cereal with reduced sugar. But it didn't sell, as customers didn't like the taste as much. This is an example of a Think challenge. The manufacturer can't respond to such a significant market change by tinkering with their existing products. They need to get curious and think differently.

So what?

As business leaders there are three things you need to be aware of in these situations.

One is bad news, but the other two are good.

First the bad news.

1. If the culture is not supportive, the coaching done at the individual level will be less effective.

Professional coaches call this "the impact of the system." What it means is that it is far more difficult for an individual to change if those around them are still behaving in an old way. For example, if one manager in the bank tried to be immensely customer focused in a culture where profit is prioritized, he'd probably start getting pressure from his peers, and probably his boss, if his sales numbers slipped. And if the measures didn't support his change in behavior, he'd face increasing pressure to revert.

And the good news.

2. A leader's impact should not be underestimated.

The good news about us being social animals is that we are also programmed to copy and learn from our leaders. So, if you, as the leader, or as the coach of a leader, consciously role model a new behavior or challenge the current mindset, the impact will be huge. Others will take notice and will be more likely to follow.

3. The same tools that work for individuals work for businesses too.

Everything we've taught you in this book works beyond the individual level. So, you can try the tools out with your team too.

In the next section we'll tell four stories and look at how the tools in this book can help teams or groups make particular mindset shifts.

Story One: Be – Becoming Resourceful

Now imagine the finance department we discussed earlier. Eric is its leader. The business wants to restructure the department to separate out and offshore the transactional work, allowing them to focus on advising and providing data to the business. Eric thinks this is a great opportunity because his team will be taking on more interesting and strategic work.

But he notices that his team is becoming increasingly anxious. They hold back on handing over work to the new offshore center and keep finding excuses to do it themselves. He overhears conversations strongly opposing the move.

Eric recognizes that his team is not resourceful around the change. They are anxious, and this is showing up as resistance. This is a Be shift. The finance team is in the box. This also tells Eric what the right tool is, and the tool for coaching people out of the box is ETC.

Eric therefore calls a team meeting. He starts the meeting by saying that he's heard that people have some concerns about the change, and he wants to have a chance to explore them.

E – EMOTION

You may remember the Emotion part of the process is all about expressing feelings and articulating the self-talk that lies behind them. By making self-talk explicit it enables the rational mind to look at it more objectively. This is true for groups too.

So, Eric asks the group which elements of change they feel strongly about. And in each case, he asks the group what their concerns are.

For example, one team member says, "I feel strongly about us handling the invoicing overseas."

Eric says, "What is your concern here?"

The team member says, "Mistakes will be made; our customers will get frustrated and will blame us."

Another adds in, "But you won't need us, so we'll have a much smaller team and won't be able to help."

And so on.

This is clearly the E stage of ETC. Eric is asking the team to share their emotions and to express their self-talk. In each case he simply captures the concern on a flip chart using the team members' exact words.

T – TRUTH

You may remember that the T stage is the opportunity to explore what the truth is behind the self-talk. Having established their trust, you have solid ground on which to make a decision.

So, Eric takes each of the key concerns in turn. He then gently explores each one. *What are the facts here? What has happened so far? What could we do?* By taking each concern and gently probing to find out the truth, he turns a long list of anxieties into a few tangible problems.

For example, for the comment, "Mistakes will be made; our customers will get frustrated and will blame us," Eric asks, "What have we seen so far that is raising this concern for us?" The team members give one or two examples, such as, "The overseas office took two days to respond to a query."

After a short discussion of examples, he says, "So, do we know that the overseas office will make mistakes?"

"No—we don't know for sure," replies the team reluctantly. "And why do we care?" asks Eric. "Because we've got standards," replies one team member. "These are our customers and we care about them," replies another.

This is the T stage of ETC. The manager, Eric, is coaching the team to find the truth in their concerns.

And the T stage is the truth to the assumptions that the team holds about the situation that is keeping the team in the box.

C – CHOICE

The C stage is about positive choice. In other words, given the truth discussed, what choices can be made?

In this case the Eric coaches the team to make a positive choice.

"So, if we care about quality and want to maintain standards and have seen some early examples that the overseas office may not have the same standards, what choices do we want to make?"

"Let's feedback our concerns."

"More than that, why don't we mentor them—why couldn't one of us fly out there for a few weeks and coach them?"

As you can see, the C stage should result in tangible ideas for action that can then be agreed upon.

Eric followed the same process for the other concerns raised and left the meeting with a new commitment from the team to engage with the change in a more positive way.

This is the same ETC process we've taught you to use with coachees—in our extensive experience, it works with businesses and organizations too.

Story Two: Relate – A Merger of Two Confectionary Companies

A big multinational confectionary business bought an established local mint candy manufacturer. The cultures couldn't have been more different. The local mint candy manufacturer was all about tradition. It was hierarchical and proud of its heritage. They saw themselves as artisans. They saw the multinational as being "all about the money," "cutting corners," and "not caring about people." By contrast, the big multinational was fast moving and modern. They saw the local candy manufacturer's leaders as "conservative," "hierarchical," and not "focused on the customer."

As you can imagine, the tension was beginning to undermine the early stages of the merger.

The leader of the process, Karina, saw the problem and correctly diagnosed that this was a Relate mindset shift. This told her the process to use—See, Hear, Speak.

Step 1 – See

You'll remember that this is all about letting go of biases and getting into the shoes of the other person.

Karina sat down with key leaders from each business. In each case she asked them to imagine they were from the other business. So, for example, she asked the leaders from the local mint sweet maker to imagine they were leaders from the multinational. She then asked, "Now imagine this group of leaders looking at you. What do you think they see? What judgments are they making?"

This led to an active conversation. Karina then asked, "And how do you imagine they are feeling?"

The leaders from the mint sweet company started saying, "Frustrated," "They probably feel angry that we aren't making an effort to understand their processes," and so on.

As you can see, through this dialogue Karina was asking each leadership group to get into the shoes of the other, inviting greater empathy and connection.

Step 2 – Hear

You'll remember this is all about letting the other person feel heard.

Karina then set up a joint meeting. The rules were that this meeting was to find out about the other party's experience. There were to be no solutions and no feedback. All leaders had to do was listen, ask great questions, and reflect back. Having piqued people's interest with the See stage, they were keen to check it out. The meeting went really well, and each group became fascinated about understanding the other's culture.

Step 3 – Speak

Speak is then about sharing your message.

Karina then asked each group to think, knowing what they know now, about the one commitment they would make to help the integration succeed, and what would be the one request they would have of leaders from the other business.

For example, the leaders from the mint sweet business came up with a commitment to be open to adopting some of the new, more modern approaches of the multinational. They asked that the multinational leaders would spend time understanding the history and approach that made their business so special.

By using the See-Hear-Speak structure, Karina was able to coach two sets of business leaders into a very different relationship.

Story Three: Inspire – A Group of Inner-City Schools

Carol was recruited by the British government to support a group of 25 inner-city schools that underachieved academically. The poor results were accompanied by low expectations.

When she took on the role, Carol recognized the need for the Inspire shift, as she saw many dedicated, hardworking school leaders working long hours to solve problems and keep the system running—but little shared leadership of the need to change the overall attainment culture.

Knowing it was the Inspire shift, Carol mirrored the visioning process.

I - Important

In the first meetings she focused on asking the schools to share what they did best and their most inspiring stories. This uncovered some amazing work and some outstanding capabilities. But is also helped uncover the core values of the teaching staff in the area. For example, there was a deep value around ensuring opportunity for all.

C - Change

In the second set of meetings, she invited the team to imagine themselves five years in the future and visualize what had been achieved. These were inspiring conversations, and the team emerged with an overall purpose statement and three pillars of their turnaround strategy.

E – Experiments

Finally, she set up a third meeting and, given the vision and the pillars, asked the school leaders to set up working groups looking at particular projects.

The results were outstanding, and Carol's work was acknowledged by the British government as being the most successful scheme of its type in the country.

She has helped the schools make the Inspire shift, owning and shaping their own change agenda.

Story Four: A Fast-Food Franchise

As with many fast-food companies, this one was a franchise. In other words, restaurants were owned by individual investors who paid a fee in order to use the brand and serve its products.

The challenge for Steve, who was managing director for a large geographic area, was how to persuade franchisees to see that customers were changing, and they were no longer comfortable simply buying the old processed formula. For example, customer focus groups were telling him that they wanted to personalize their sandwich, to create better-for-me options, and to avoid lines. But his teams struggled to convince enough franchisees to make the investment required to respond to these trends.

For several years, his teams had been presenting innovative solutions to change the customer experience, but he kept getting pushback and resistance from the franchise owners who were reluctant to make the investment.

This is a classic Think challenge. The franchisees are stuck in green thinking about the way their business works, and it can be easy for the head office to simply get frustrated with them.

Steve decided to use the Breakthrough Thinking Cycle. At first in their biannual franchisee meeting, he asked the franchise owners to share their concerns and frustrations. Of course, within this list the franchise owners were also seeing different demands and needs from customers and experiencing competition from new, more modern fast-food businesses.

Looking Up

He then worked with them to frame two inquiry questions from their frustrations. One was, "How do we continue to compete and win customers as customers become more demanding?"

Looking Out

For the second half of the day he then invited different stakeholders in (customers, employees, local community representatives) and arranged for the franchise owners to spend time listening to their ideas and needs.

At the end of the day the franchise owners began coming up with ideas for how to respond to the new market. Some of these ideas were the same as the ones the head office had already considered—others were new. But the difference was that now the franchisees had broken out of one river of thinking and were thinking differently. This meant that it was no longer the head office selling solutions to them, but them feeling like partners in thinking about how the business should respond.

This allowed for the rest of the cycle to work successfully in generating new insights and solutions.

So, what does this mean?

The good news is that by having read this book, you know how to change culture and mindset within your business. The same tools work with teams or with stakeholders in the business. By coaching or facilitating them through the processes in this book, you can help change organizational mindsets.

This is immensely powerful. Books have been written about culture and culture change. But at its heart, culture is shaped by the beliefs that are common to it—through mindset. And as we now know, mindsets can be changed.

This doesn't negate the other tools of change management. For example, rewards or structures can have a big impact on the likelihood of these techniques working. But it does give you a toolkit to do the toughest part of change—changing mindset.

PART THREE

Going Deeper:
Understanding
Mindset Change

Chapter 6

Why Each
Mindset Is Different

W HEN WE FIRST STARTED postulating this approach, we posed two challenges:

Challenge One: Is There really a Psychological Difference Between the Four Shifts? Why is each mindset different?

Challenge Two: How Valid Are the Four Areas? Why the Four Areas?

In this chapter we'll explore both of these questions.

Challenge One: Why is each mindset different?

Roberto Assagioli

Assagioli was an Italian psychiatrist, working with contemporaries Sigmund Freud and Carl Jung. He had a great model for understanding the mind, and therefore it is a good source for understanding why each mindset is different.

Assagioli created one of the most comprehensive models of the psyche, often referred to as "Assagioli's egg."[1]

We have drawn on his model loosely to explain mindsets, using our version of the psyche. Our model gives a map of the mindsets we access and experience, which will then allow you to differentiate the types of conversations that change the mindset.

Let's start with understanding each section in our simplified model of the psyche.

Lower Self: The mindsets here are not yet fully conscious, and they center around old beliefs that are assumed over time. For example, the leader who wanted to give more feedback may have a belief that feedback will hurt the relationship. While he may want to change his behavior of giving feedback, in practice it will be overridden by this mindset. This mindset inhibits sustainable change in behavior.

Higher Self: The mindsets here are not yet fully conscious, and they center around connecting with meaning, purpose, and values. This is the higher self—how one aspires to be. By making this conscious, you can coach others around their choices and lead in a way that truly expresses their higher aspirations.

Conscious Self: This is what a coachee is aware of—what is happening now and what they can most easily access in memory. It is the part they can access to make their day-to-day decisions. When a coachee becomes conscious of a mindset, it will be part of the conscious self.

The Ecosystem: Imagine coaching someone in an organizational culture where junior staff don't challenge senior staff. It is normal, as social animals, to adopt or be impacted by the behaviors and beliefs of leaders within the culture. These are mindsets in the ecosystem. So mindsets in the collective often impact the unconscious mindsets of the coachee. You'll see that the Think and Relate conversations are ways you can, as a coach, help your coachees be effective in the wider ecosystem.

The dotted lines throughout the diagram indicate that no section of the model is isolated from other sections—a coachee will move among them day to day. For example, in one moment, a coachee may be connected to their values mindset from the higher self, and in another moment, they may react to a colleague from an old, lower-self mindset of anger and

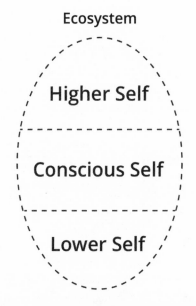

Figure 6-1: A simplified model of the psyche

judgment. In this model, development is about becoming more aware of all of these sections. As a coachee becomes more aware, for example, by becoming conscious of their values in the higher-self sector, they have access to greater choice, possibility, and freedom. Their middle conscious expands upward, downward, and outward.

One trap you can get caught in is thinking that the higher self is good and the lower self is bad. This is not how we hold it. All aspects have value in them. When we bring consciousness to them, the potential that is locked in the mindsets of the higher or lower self is released. But when the mindsets are not conscious, that's when the potential that lies in that area of the self is missed.

Assagioli referred to this integration journey of all aspects of the psyche as psychosynthesis.

This simple model of the self is a great way to understand the four areas of mindset shift.

BE

The Be conversations are about bringing awareness to the lower-self mindsets, thereby allowing a coachee to have more choice over their state. This is because the unconscious beliefs in the lower self drive the coachee's behavior. But because they are beyond awareness, your coachee can't edit them.

All "Be" conversations are about expanding the conscious self to become aware of the lower self and hence enable the coachee to choose a resourceful response to the situation.

Take the simple example where I coached a member of our team in delivering a presentation. She was nervous because it was her first time presenting. Through coaching, she recognized the lower-self mindsets that were creating the nervousness: "What if I'm not good enough?" "What if I can't remember what to say? I will be embarrassed." Simply expressing her concerns allowed her conscious mind to challenge them. By making her fears conscious, her conscious self could choose to operate free from these beliefs. She grew in confidence and was able

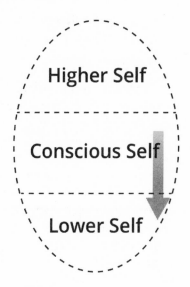

Figure 6-2: Be mindset shifts

to deliver the presentation with energy and passion.

BE shifts.

Conscious self expands downward.

The impact on leadership is significant: our coachees will be able to self-manage better, reduce stress, improve their well-being, see with more perspective, and increase their creativity.

Thus, the heart of our Be conversations is about expanding the conscious self toward the lower self.

RELATE

Our Relate conversations increase awareness of mindsets outside the psyche—toward the mindset of others in the ecosystem. The coachee's mindset also expands outward in the process—they have greater conscious awareness of others. They are better able to navigate other people and the environment.

> **RELATE** shifts.
>
> Conscious self expands to learn from others' worlds.

For example, a direct report had a strong disagreement with a colleague. The mindset toward the colleague was, "They are wrong; how could they fail to approve a budget for a training that I needed?" He was annoyed and upset, and this could be observed when the two people were together.

What helped the direct report was recognizing that the colleague had a mindset of their own, and inviting the direct report to see if they could be open to the other's mindset and perspective. He was able to understand that the colleague was simply trying their best to keep within budget, an expectation in their role. It was not personal. By understanding and empathizing with others, the direct report was able to

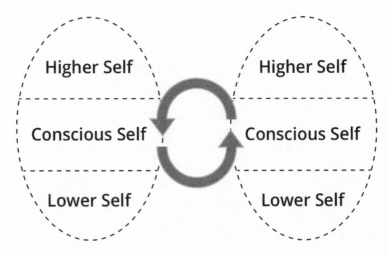

Figure 6-3: Relate mindset shifts

change—he expanded his own mindset to embrace the mindset of the other. As a result, he could now approach the conversation with less defensiveness, and they were able to come up with a solution that was much more win-win for both.

INSPIRE

By contrast, the Inspire conversations are essentially all about tapping into our coachee's higher self. By tapping into their sense of purpose, higher meaning, and values, you are able to

INSPIRE shifts.

Conscious self expands upwards.

help them clarify who they really want to be and the difference they want to make.

In this way, the coaching is expanding the conscious self toward the higher self.

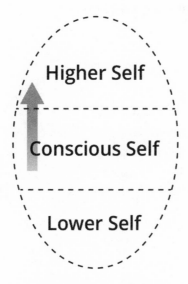

Figure 6-4: Inspire mindset shifts

As our coachee becomes more conscious of their values, dreams, and hopes, they can choose to lead and respond to the challenges in front of them in a very different way.

THINK

The Think conversations are also about expanding outward, but this time expanding outward into the ecosystem—the wider world—and challenging mindsets about this.

For example, former Starbucks CEO Howard Schultz challenged the view or mindset in the United States that coffee was a commodity. He was inspired by the Romantic mindset surrounding coffee in Italy. He created the Starbucks brand, a mindset shift about the coffee shop, called the

> **THINK** shifts.
>
> Conscious self expands to learn from the broader environment and context.

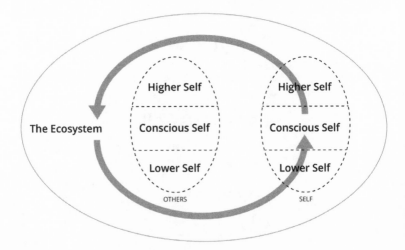

Figure 6-5: Think mindset shifts

coffee house: "a third place between work and home."[2] This view of the coffee experience took over the world—it's now a multibillion-dollar market.

The heart of all innovation involves challenging the coachee's familiar views of the world—often mindsets that are in the ecosystem or culture—by getting curious, listening, and creating new possibilities. The Think conversation is about expanding the conscious self toward the wider ecosystem.

Using the model of the self, we can see that each shift is different in that they open up awareness in distinctly different sectors of the psyche. It also then stands to reason that each area will require different coaching interventions to support the mindset shift related to that sector.

Challenge Two: Why the four areas?

The best way to answer this is to see how our four areas correlate with other great authors' work. We will look at them in turn.

Daniel Goleman

Daniel Goleman is a well-known writer and influential leader in the field of emotional intelligence in the workplace. His research has shown the benefits of developing emotional intelligence, or EQ, for our leaders. For example, his latest model of emotional intelligence has four dimensions:

- Self-awareness
- Self-management
- Social awareness
- Relationship management

He has outlined 18 competencies under these dimensions.[3]

We see that our Be conversation aligns with the development of self-awareness and self-management, so that the coachee becomes aware of the times they are in the box and using the ETC tool to manage their state. The mindset shifts in the Relate conversation align with the development of social awareness and relationship management. In other words, Goleman's work appears to highlight the importance of the Be and Relate shifts on performance.

Peter Senge

Peter Senge is one of the most influential thought leaders in the field of individual and organizational development today. His view on individual development is set within the framework that organizations that learn will have the ultimate competitive advantage.[4]

A learning organization is one that does not depend only on senior management to do all the thinking for an entire corporation. Rather, it invites and challenges leaders to access their inner resource and potential to build their own community based on the collective will to learn.

His seminal work, *The Fifth Discipline*, describes five disciplines that must be mastered by leaders when introducing learning into an organization. These are

1. Systems thinking: This relates to the ability to see the big picture, to see patterns rather than viewing changes as isolated events. It is about seeing that we are an interconnecting whole in the way we operate, solve business challenges, and act.

2. Personal mastery: This begins by becoming committed to lifelong learning. This is about being realistic, truthful, and committed to realization of potential.

3. Mental models: This discipline is about learning to let go of our mental models—our deeply held belief structures and generalizations—and seeing how they dramatically impact the way we operate in our

lives. True change can only take place when we are open and free from these mental models.

4. Building shared visions: In today's world, visions cannot be dictated from the top down. This discipline begins with personal visions of individual employees. Creating a shared vision has the power to bring an organization together, fostering a commitment to the long term.

5. Team learning: It is a process of developing the ability to work together to create desired results through the instigation of a learning mindset.[5]

Our four shifts are clearly aligned with Senge's five disciplines: our Be conversation unlocks shifts in personal mastery and mental models, our Relate conversation unlocks shifts in team learning, our Think conversation unlocks shifts in systems thinking, and our Inspire conversation unlocks shifts in building shared visions.

James Kouzes and Barry Posner

James Kouzes is the Executive Fellow of Leadership at the Santa Clara University Leavey School of Business and is cited as one of the 12 best executive educators by the *Wall Street Journal*. Barry Posner is the Accolti Endowed Professor of Leadership in the Leavey School of Business. Together they have coauthored more than a dozen leadership books, including *The Leadership Challenge*, which has sold over two million copies worldwide.

In this book they outline their five practices of exemplary leadership, based on research on thousands of leaders:

1. Model the way: To earn credibility, leaders must clarify their values and express these values to everyone in the organization. They should also serve as an example to others in their commitment to

their values. The commitments required for this practice are to "clarify values" and "set the example."

2. Inspire a shared vision: This has two commitments. First, purpose. Second, to "enlist others" to make it a reality.

3. Challenge the process: The two commitments for this practice are to "search for opportunities" and "experiment and take risks," enabling the organization to continually grow, innovate, and improve.

4. Enable others to act: The commitments with this practice are to "foster collaboration" and "strengthen others," which recognizes that success occurs through teams that are collaborating with individual accountability.

5. Encourage the heart: This is about uplifting spirits of people on the team, with commitments to "recognize contributions" and "celebrate values and victories."[6]

Here we see strong alignment with four areas of mindset shift: "modeling the way" and "inspiring a shared vision" align with the Be and Inspire shifts (specifically, Be, which is about making conscious choices as a leader, and Inspire, which focuses on clarifying our values and expressing it through a vision that can be shared with others); "challenge the process" maps to our Think shift; our Relate mindset shift aligns with the last two practices of "enabling others to act" and "encouraging the heart."

Howard Gardner

Gardner argued that human beings have a range of intelligences and that IQ was not the only assessment measure for smartness, seeing such assessments as "one-dimensional."[7] He also saw that intelligences develop, and that each individual had a unique combination of intelligences across the spectrum, which included musical and spiritual intelligence. Three intelligences from Gardner's work that are key to leadership are outlined here.

- Logical mathematical intelligence consists of our capacity to analyze problems, investigate, detect patterns, reason deductively, and think logically.

- Intrapersonal intelligence consists of our capacity to understand oneself—feelings, fears, drives, and motivations. It involves the ability to use such information to regulate ourselves.

- Interpersonal intelligence consists of our capacity to understand the intentions, motivations, and desires of other people. It enables us to work effectively with other people.

There is clearly a direct correlation between these fundamental leadership intelligences and our four shifts (with extensive research showing the beneficial impact of developing these intelligences): our Be shift is concerned with developing our intrapersonal intelligence; the Inspire shift develops our intrapersonal intelligence (understanding what motivates ourselves through our values); the Think shift develops our logical mathematical intelligence; the Relate shift develops our interpersonal intelligence.

Gardner offers us a lens on the four areas, or quadrants, of conversation: each quadrant is a line of intelligence, which grows as our mindset shifts and expands. Thus, different leaders will have strengths in each, and it will be important when coaching a leader that we identify the right area of the shift for them. For example, we know some leaders are very good at innovation, but they may be poor in their people skills—the *Think intelligence* will be strong, but more shifts may be needed in the *Relate intelligence*.

Conclusion

Clearly there is increasing awareness that effective behavior and impactful leadership are critical enablers of business performance.[1]

The areas Be, Think, Relate, and Inspire are clearly key to achieving this, and they are uniquely different. They each focus on a different area of ourselves and leadership. Thus, coaching them requires a different approach—once we identify the area of shift, we can vary our coaching approach with greater precision to meet the change that our coachee wishes to make.

Chapter 7

The Psychology
of Mindset

THIS CHAPTER GOES A BIT DEEPER for those who want to look further "under the hood" and explore what it really takes to change mindset.

Transformation and change are buzzwords in the world of coaching right now. But do we really know what it takes to change mindset? Imagine you are in a negative state. If I or any other coach said, "Well, just change your mind about it," I don't think that would do it.

In our four conversations, we have shown ways of changing mindset successfully. But what is the "secret sauce" of mindset change that resides within these conversations? If we can unravel the key elements, we can then develop greater mastery in coaching others with their mindset. This is the subject of this chapter.

In this chapter we will

- Understand the five key principles, the secret sauce to changing mindsets (we will draw on the four conversations as examples);

- Explore how you can develop mastery in transforming mindsets in each of the conversations; and

- Look at four key barriers to change and how to overcome them. If it were simple, our coachees would all be changing mindsets. Of course, there are barriers in the way, as you probably know from your own life. We will look at some ways of working with those barriers.

As the title says, this chapter is a chance to look further "under the hood." You don't need it to have the four conversations. But for those who want to attain mastery, this chapter will help.

A simple metaphor for change

Let's leave coaching conversations for a moment and think about transformation itself. Take a moment to reflect broadly on this question: what is transformation or change?

Looking at the language *trans* and *form*, it is about changing the form. In nature, we have the lovely metaphor of the caterpillar turning into a butterfly that we can learn from. The caterpillar does not automatically change into a butterfly. There is a period of transition in the pupa—a process of letting go of the old and transitioning into the new.

Let's look at an example to connect back to coaching conversations. I coached a person who was obviously flustered, having just come out of a meeting with her boss. "I really messed up and my boss was irate," she said, exasperated. "I know I am in the box, but I am feeling really upset and annoyed with myself at the moment."

As we explored the situation in coaching, she realized that her self-talk was exaggerated.

- She hadn't "messed up." What had happened was that she hadn't known the answer to one particular question.

- She didn't know that her boss was angry. Her boss had raised his eyebrows in response to her saying she didn't have an answer to a question—he may have been curious, confused, or simply having a twitch in his eyebrow.

As we explored what had gone on for her, not only did she see the limitations of her self-talk, but she also, with the help of her Realist, began accepting that she'd already proven her worth as a leader.

The trivial incident of the eyebrow helped her realize that she was much too worried about how others saw her, and she had no need to be this way. This allowed her to find a new level of confidence that she could now apply to many other conversations. A whole new worldview—all from a twitching eyebrow!

You have probably recognized that this is the mindset shift in the Be conversation. We could say that the old mindset or worldview was like the caterpillar. This is the in-the-box mindset. This mindset was governing her experience, interpreting the situation with assumptions that were not actually true. The new worldview or mindset was her butterfly. She was seeing the world more truthfully, from the mindset of her Realist. She had changed the form of her mindset. Her world actually looked different. She had transformed her experience not only of this situation but of many future ones. Of course, this required conscious practice. This is the heart of all the mindset-changing conversations: transforming an old mindset to a new one.

If we extend this further, we actually have access to many mindsets.

Neuroscience confirms that we have multiple mindsets and worldviews (sometimes called subpersonalities) available in the moment that make up the sense of self. Each subpersonality is a combination of thoughts, feelings, and physiology.[1]

Why is it helpful to think of our mindsets as subpersonalities? A coachee can then name or imagine the subpersonality as a character; by seeing it, they are less gripped by it in the moment. You may have seen the movie *Inside Out*, where the young girl in the movie is depicted as having five "subpersonalities" inside her, and these personalities navigate her reactions, choices, and behavior.[2] These subpersonalities are five depictions of her inner mindsets. Sometimes they are aligned and sometimes they are in conflict. It is a great way of understanding what actually happens in our experience.

We can see this clearly when, let's say, you are driving a car, and someone cuts in front of you suddenly. On one day you may experience feelings of rage, a physiological response of heart racing, and thoughts about how inconsiderate the other driver is and how you might plan your revenge. You are overtaken by a particular subpersonality. On another day you may respond differently, maybe more calmly, with a mindset that is not perturbed when being cut off. A different mindset or subpersonality will be "driving" your experience.

Coming back to the example of the woman who was triggered by the raised eyebrows of her boss, we could say that she was overtaken by a particular subpersonality, one that looked to others for approval. On another day (and certainly, she had this experience too), another subpersonality could be present, and she just would not be affected by what others were thinking about her. This could be the Realist subpersonality.

Tying this together with the metaphor of the butterfly, we are letting go of one subpersonality with a particular mindset and embracing a new subpersonality or mindset. Our outlook or worldview has transformed.

Through the four tools, ETC, See-Hear-Speak, ICE, and the Breakthrough Thinking Process, we effectively coach to shift from one subpersonality to another, expanding our capacity for choice.

All the transformational tools are about changing worldviews or mindsets: a limited one to a more expanded one. Why is that important? Well, we have seen that a coachee is then able to access more perspectives and choices, having a different impact on others and the business.

1. BE conversations: The coachee changes from their triggered subpersonality to their Realist subpersonality using the ETC tool.

2. RELATE conversations: The coachee changes from a subpersonality rooted in their view of the world to one that is more empathic and understanding of the other, using the Presence Triangle tool in the See step. They continue to expand this mindset when they Hear and Speak.

3. INSPIRE conversations: The coachee changes from a task-oriented subpersonality to an inspired and values-driven subpersonality using the ICE process.

4. THINK conversations: The coachee moves from their usual way of problem solving or their habitual subpersonality to a curious and innovative subpersonality using the Breakthrough Thinking Cycle. In other words, they shift from the green-thinking subpersonality to the blue-thinking subpersonality.

These are the shifts from the caterpillar to the butterfly perspectives across each of the conversations. Each new subpersonality comes with its own worldview. As we have said at the start, the mindset will be expressed as behaviors, thereby impacting others and work results.

Whilst there are many subpersonalities and mindsets, this book is about the four overarching mindsets shifts that come up over and over again. Each person will have their own version of a judge or pessimist, for example, but the shift to their version of the Realist is the same.

With this understanding, we can look at what this means for successfully transforming the mindset in coaching. How can you master the tools? You can't simply tell someone to move from the old worldview (the caterpillar in our metaphor) to the new worldview (the butterfly) without considering the process of change.

Mastering the Tools

What helped the woman in the last example of the Be conversation shift? Even though this client knew she was in the box, there is a big step from knowing she was triggered by her manager to finding a more confident and assured personality. It certainly wasn't enough to point out she was in the box. It wasn't even enough to help rationally put the raised eyebrow in perspective. What turns the trivial detail of a raised eyebrow into an opportunity to change something much more significant?

Think of your own examples. What helps you look at a situation from one perspective to a completely different one? Looking at another example from the Relate shift, imagine you are in the midst of a heated debate with someone—any urge to collaborate and influence has simply gone out of the window. What will help you to see and hear the other person in the heat of the moment? What will help you to step into the other person's shoes when that is the last thing on your mind?

Coming back to our coachees, what will support them to shift from their limited mindsets or subpersonalities to engaging a more liberated mindset or subpersonality—whether that mindset has to do with their resourcefulness from the Realist perspective (Be), seeing the world from the other's perspective (Relate), engaging values in creating their direction and vision (Inspire), or stepping back and accessing their innovative blue-thinking mindset (Think)—especially in those critical moments where the impact of transforming the mindset might be very significant?

With the understanding of transformation and subpersonalities, we will explore five dimensions that support this transformation.

It is worth saying this at the outset: each of the five dimensions of mastery takes time. Take your time in learning and experimenting, choosing the dimension that piques your interest in developing your skills further before moving onto the next one.

The Five Dimensions

Dimension One: Tap into their real and specific experience

In the Be, Relate, and Inspire conversations, you invite the coachee to really experience a specific scenario live in the moment and use present tense, rather than talk generically. For example,

- In Be, the coachee is invited to identify and experience a specific trigger in the moment or a specific time they were connected to their Realist in the moment.

- In Relate, you ask the coachee to share a real example of the specific moment where the conflict or misalignment occurred while using the Presence Triangle tool, rather than talking generically about why that relationship is not working or what is wrong with it.

- In Inspire, you ask the coachee to truly imagine and step into a specific moment in the future when they write their letter, rather than talk about the future generically from a distance. You then coach them to face both their current reality and desired reality in the rubber band exercise.

- We can also apply this principle to the Think conversation: you can explore the specific situations and moments where the coachee is frustrated about the business to identify their inquiry question. You could, where it's useful, ask them to connect with a specific time in their experience when they were in their blue-thinking mindset.

There are three reasons why this is important.

The first reason, which applies to the Be and Relate conversations, is that getting specific with a real situation really helps to understand and make the "caterpillar," or subpersonality, conscious before a coachee can let go of it.

There are many people we have worked with who haven't even realized that they are, for example, caught by their underlying assumptions, including the self-talk from their Pessimist and Judge. For them it is just normal. By imagining the specific moment where they are in the box, they are much more clearly able to see the patterns and assumptions that are driving them when they are caught by that mindset. The coachee then opens up the possibility of allowing a different perspective. Otherwise, they will carry on in the cycle of the self-talk.

The fairy tale of the princess and the pea describes it well. If you don't know it, a princess was trying to sleep, but unbeknownst to her, she was lying on a pea. The discomfort meant she couldn't sleep. To solve the problem, she added another mattress. When that didn't work, she added another mattress, and this continued until someone took her back to the first mattress and showed her that there was a pea at the source of her discomfort. This is what happens when a coachee is caught by a limiting mindset: they carry on without being aware of what is causing their discomfort. By working in the moment, you can unravel the source of the trigger—their mindset.

By working with real experience, the coachee is able to access the entire experience of that subpersonality or worldview when it is active—the coachee gets to consciously experience the source of the trigger (the "pea"), and therefore can let go of it.

Turning to the second reason, for a moment let's turn back in time to an important discovery of Sigmund Freud. You may know him from his work in popularizing the fact that we have an unconscious. However, another insight came from his work with trauma. He found that by reexperiencing the traumatic event (which was later done using hypnosis), the trauma would release.[3] Now, the people we work with are not traumatized! And we are not planning to do therapy with our colleagues. But the principle still applies—if we experience the moment of trigger (for example, the trigger moment of going in the box or when we go into conflict), it becomes much easier to let go of the subpersonality we are caught by. In the moment, if you can work with the feelings, thoughts, and physiological sensations of the coachee's subpersonality (with their permission, of course) there is a much better chance of them being able to release it and let go.

We now understand more about this from a neuroscience perspective. When a coachee is triggered, their brain is hijacked by their emotions and reactions, sending signals across the body to fight, flight, or freeze. The behavior correspondingly reflects their state. By describing the experience autobiographically with real experiences, the coachee is able to process their experience. The nervous system relaxes once again. They then have the capacity to make more conscious choices.

In other words, if a particular subpersonality is activated, a coachee can't skip it. They have to face it and experience it before they can let it go.

To use the model of the psyche from chapter 6, you are effectively first bringing the mindset to the awareness of the conscious self in order to become aware of it, and then let it go. This is key in the process of transformation—experiencing and letting go of the subpersonality before the new one can emerge.

Furthermore, you can also help the coachee by guiding their experience of the new subpersonality or mindset in the moment too—you help them to lay down new neural pathways that, with practice, become hard wired.

The third reason for experiencing the specific moment is that the coachee is able to see and access the qualities in the subpersonality—even the ones they may call negative. If you remember, in chapter 6 we talked about the fact that lower-self mindsets aren't bad. They have value in them. That is what we are referring to here. For example, the quality in our pessimistic subpersonality might be our capacity to alert us to future problems. The quality in our critical subpersonality might be discernment.

Imagine, instead, if a coachee wanted to get rid of their critic subpersonality and always be optimistic. They would have quite a skewed perception about life. Rather, it is helpful to see the value in the critic—the capacity to discern where things could be improved. It is only when a coachee gets caught by believing the exaggerations and drama of the critic subpersonality, rather than listening to the value and quality, that it becomes a problem. We have seen this in the Think conversation—there is value in the frustrations, and if the coachee can become conscious of all of their mindsets or subpersonalities, they can turn them into creative opportunities. All subpersonalities are powerful potentials that can be harnessed when the coachee makes them conscious in the moment.

Hints/Tips

Questions that you can ask the coachee when connecting with a specific and real moment include these:

Be (ETC): When did that trigger last occur? What specifically happened? Have you got a specific example of when you went into the box?

Imagine you can see the trigger moment on a movie screen playing in front of you. What are you seeing or feeling (in the present tense)? Take yourself back there—what is the experience like as you imagine that situation now? How are you feeling as you describe the situation?

When was the last time you experienced yourself in your Realist? Imagining yourself in that moment, what is the experience of the Realist? How is that experience in your physiology? What is important in the self-talk—the value that might be expressed here?

Relate (Presence Triangle exercise): When was the last time that conflict occurred? Now, imagine you can see the other person in front of you. What are you seeing or feeling? What are you telling yourself about them? How do you notice yourself responding? What about your perspective might contain some truth that you wish to keep? How might you share that truth without judgment?

Inspire (letter from the future): Pick a specific moment in the future. Tell me a future moment that is significant to you. Imagine yourself as if you are in the future moment now. How do you feel? What is the experience like? What do you see around you?

Think (Breakthrough Thinking Cycle): When was the last time you felt frustrated about how things were working in the business? Imagine yourself in that moment now. As you look at the situation in the moment, where are you feeling frustrated? What are your thoughts? What is frustrating you? What do you notice frustrates others?

More generally you can ask questions like these: what image, character, or metaphor describes you in this moment? What are its behaviors? What are the typical thought patterns associated with it? What are its needs? What are its values? These questions allow the coachee to really become conscious of their subpersonality so that they can catch it next time it is active.

Dimension Two: The magic of feelings

Working only on the rational level does not create lasting change. For example, in a disagreement, a coachee can rationally tell themselves that there is another point of view, but still find themselves, in the moment, fighting for their position at all costs.

Each subpersonality, or worldview, has the components of thoughts, feelings, and physiological responses. Talking about the triggered subpersonality is not enough.

Think about that situation when being cut off by another driver—in the moment, you will be feeling frustration and anger. You'll experience a racing heart and a shortness of breath.

What we find in practice is that if we don't engage with the feelings of the coachee, they are likely to be vulnerable to return to their original state.

We all know that sometimes talking about feelings when a coachee is upset can help them to let go and feel lighter. There is even a cliché in the West: a problem shared is a problem halved. Human beings sometimes need to express the feeling in order to let it go. It is much easier to let go of a subpersonality by first expressing the feelings associated with it. This is the magic. It is the power of emotional intelligence.

And it is healthy to do so, especially when caught in some strong emotion around a particular situation. Sometimes a coachee will need to rant when someone has crossed a line before they can give helpful feedback to the person. This is OK. When consciously done, they don't then have to sabotage the relationship in the process. They can let go and then return to the situation from a more centered aspect of themselves. Questions like, "How do you feel?" "How are you experiencing that right now?" or "What's going on for you?" can be really helpful, combined with a good listening ear.

From a neuroscience perspective, the emotional arousal a person experiences in situations like conflict or not being at their best can be significantly calmed just by expressing them in words.

Alex Korb did an fMRI study titled "Putting Feelings into Words." fMRI, or functional magnetic resonance imaging, measures brain activity by detecting changes associated with blood flow. It is an innovative way for measuring objective data about the brain. In the study, participants were shown pictures that caused a reaction in the emotional center in the brain, the amygdala. But when they named the emotion, another part of the brain, the ventrolateral prefrontal cortex, became active and reduced the emotional amygdala reactivity. "Consciously recognizing the emotions reduced their impact.... [D]escribe an emotion in just a word or two, and it helps to reduce the emotion," the author found.[4]

Many people believe that it is possible to put a lid on their feelings, in the hope that they go away. This never works. We know this because, after a stressful day at work or a trigger, it is hard to stop thinking about it.

Let's look at an example of a Relate conversation. I remember recently having a disagreement with my wife. She was "reminding me" that I had forgotten to do certain house chores. I reacted: "At least ask me how my day was first! If you knew what I had gone through you wouldn't complain over something so petty." You can guess what happened next. An equally strong response back, some more to-ing and fro-ing, followed by an awkward evening. My Tasmanian Devil subpersonality was unleashed, unwilling to listen or compromise.

My brother popped in soon after the exchange. He saw me fuming, and I explained what had happened. He replied by saying, "Hey, think about it from her perspective."

While he was trying to shift my perspective or mindset with good intention, in reality I could have started an argument with him with his suggestion. I was not ready to let go of or change this perspective so quickly. I needed to vent and let off some steam. What would have helped first is to have shared my state and expressed some of my frustration, before I was ready to make space for another point of view.

If I had a few minutes to name the feelings and express my perspective, the opportunity for seeing the perspective of the other would have been far more possible. We can't go too fast with pushing the mindset to another way of looking.

Often people also try to move past their options too quickly. They try to carry on and pretend as if nothing has happened. But this is much to their peril.

David Rock cites research that shows people failed to suppress negative emotional experiences. They might have hidden them outwardly, but they found using fMRI that the emotional or "limbic system was just as aroused without suppression, and in some cases, even more aroused. Trying not to feel something doesn't work, and in some cases even backfires."[5]

Bringing in the feeling dimensions can be both helpful in relaxing the nervous system and freeing our coachees from those negative feelings, which can, in turn, impact their thinking too. Unexpressed emotions can get in the way of letting go of a subpersonality and allowing a new one in.

Hints/Tips

The simplest way to work with feelings is to listen for them.

> Ask: How do you feel about that?
> Reflect feelings: "You seem angry," "You sound sad as you say that."

Doing this—and being willing to listen to and give space to the response—is usually enough.

If you want to go further, you can work with the physiology by simply using movement. For example,

> Relate: If you are working with someone on the Presence Triangle, you can ask them to sit in three different chairs: one for themselves, one for the other person, and one for the observer. As they move through each step, they can sit in each corresponding chair and connect with what it is like to experience that position.
>
> Inspire: You can ask them to imagine a place in the room where they can see their future self, and then walk to that part of the room. They can then write their letter from there and explore their values.

When working with others, it is worth having an empathic mindset yourself: research by Korb on patients seeing doctors for a short, one-time visit for a common cold showed that they recovered one day earlier when they were met with an empathic response, and they showed an improved immune system because of empathy.[6]

A coachee is much more likely to relax and grow when they are met with a compassionate coach, especially when exploring some of their vulnerabilities.

Dimension Three: Separate the story from the facts

This is important. The data of what happens is often not the same as the coachee's interpretation of it. Put another way, when a coachee is clear on the data, then the rest of what is happening is their interpretation—their assumptions or their story about the situation.

This gives them access to the caterpillar position, the limiting subpersonality—the storyteller about the facts. Returning to the Be conversation example at the start with the woman who was triggered by her boss, she started by saying "My boss was irate." This was not data. It was her story. Asking what the fact was—his eyebrows were raised—gave clarity on the fact that she had interpreted that he was angry, and furthermore, that she had a story that he was angry with her. Once we were clear on the assumption she was making, we could look at challenging the interpretation for other possibilities. The heart of her shift involved seeing that the subpersonality of the moment was interpreting with its worldview, which then drove her state and behaviors. She was now at a place of choice.

Equally, this can be useful in working with the Presence Triangle in the Relate conversation—relationship conflict often begins with misunderstandings and misinterpretations of others, stories we tell ourselves about others. By asking for the facts of what the other said or did, we can access the story that the coachee has overlaid onto the situation. They have made the first step in beginning to change their mind about it.

Thinking back to the earlier Relate conversation example of my wife who "reminded me to do the chores," the story I told myself was that she was uncaring, unloving, unsympathetic about my day, and constantly nagging. The fact was that she had asked me why I had not done the chores yet. That fact was not quite the same as the interpretation that she doesn't love me. With the facts named clearly, I can start to see what I have done to make the situation worse—by overlying the interpretations and assumptions that come from my mindset. Not only does the story ignore the facts of what she actually said, as much as it pains me to admit, the story also does a great job of helping me to forget the fact that I had committed to her to do the chores in the first place. This clarification of the data would have facilitated the mindset shift in the See step, using the Presence Triangle exercise of the Relate conversation.

In the Think conversation, the Breakthrough Thinking Cycle certainly benefits from separating the facts from the story, particularly in the inquiry step. For example, I was coaching someone in a leadership position at a school who wanted to look at how to improve parental involvement in children's education, in a city where on average both parents were working—this was his strategic question. He looked for data through interviewing parents. At first, he was annoyed by what he was hearing, and stated, "They are just not interested in school activities." I asked him for the data—what did they actually say? He quoted specific parent comments, such as: "I am working hard, and I just want to spend time with my child in the two hours before they go to bed."

He had interpreted this statement as the parent not being interested. Instead, when we saw the data, he saw that he was misinterpreting the lack of interest—parents were, in fact, interested in spending time with their children. New ideas could now emerge—how could activities with parents be positioned in a way that highlighted the opportunity for connection with their child and their life at school? This idea may not have emerged if he had simply closed the door with the interpretation of lack of interest.

Becoming aware of our interpretation is key to changing our mindset, as each of our subpersonalities are based on particular interpretations. By separating our interpretation from facts, we get to see the subpersonality and the biases they each have. It is then easier to let go.

Hints/Tips

It can be really helpful to ask questions that seek to get to the facts. For example,

> What actually happened?
>
> If someone was watching, what would they see or hear?
>
> What were the words you actually heard?
>
> What are the facts here, and what is the narrative or story you have overlaid onto the situation or person?
>
> How can you find out what they are actually thinking or feeling about you or the situation?

Dimension Four: Don't jump into the new subpersonality!

A caterpillar can't become a butterfly without becoming a chrysalis first.

We can't just jump from the old worldview to the new—there is an intermediary step. If we think back to the metaphor of the butterfly, this is the stage of the cocoon.

If you would like some theory about this, philosopher Ken Wilber describes the process as 3-2-1.[7] The 3-2-1 is a great tool to remember this powerful process of change.

Sometimes we describe the 3-2-1 process as

> 3: blind to the new subpersonality or worldview
>
> 2: seeing the new subpersonality or worldview
>
> 1: being the new subpersonality or worldview

Inspired by his theory, from our perspective when the coachee is in the caterpillar, the new subpersonality, the butterfly, is said to be in the 3 position: we are blind to it. It is outside of awareness.

For example, in the Be conversation the coachee is in the box and caught in the feelings, thoughts, and sensations of this mindset. As a result, they are not conscious of their Realist. The Realist is in the 3 position when they are in the box. Similarly, in the Think conversation the coachee can be caught in their current (green) thinking and not aware of other perspectives—the blue-thinking subpersonality or mindset is in the 3 position, outside of awareness.

In the Relate example where I was in conflict with my wife, her perspective or mindset was in the 3 position. I didn't even want to entertain her perspective when my brother reminded me. I was identified with my point of view. This 3 position, where the new mindset is outside of awareness, is the position where I am identified with the old mindset.

After giving some voice to this position of the old mindset, the coachee can move to the 2 position. The 2 position is the power of this theory. It is hard to jump straight from the old mindset to a new one. There has to be an intermediate step.

So how do you work with this insight? It is about gently introducing the butterfly. There is a transition step. You'll notice that each conversation does this in its own way. For example, in the letter from the future in the Inspire conversation, we first ask the coachee to imagine the future self before stepping into it.

In the Presence Triangle exercise of the Relate conversation, after the coachee expresses their mindset or point of view, you first invite the coachee to step back and connect with the other person as a human being first. This is the 2 position. They are letting go of their mindset and opening to the new mindset.

In the 2 position, they are describing (and not yet being) the new subpersonality. It is like the cocoon position of the caterpillar turning into a butterfly. In the cocoon there is the breakdown or letting go of the caterpillar and the development and birth of the butterfly. You are inviting the coachee to bring the new perspective into relationship, into awareness.

In my example with my wife, I was not ready for my brother saying, "Think about her perspective." I was not ready to jump into her perspective or mindset. Instead, he might have said something like, "OK, now that you have told me what has upset you, are you up for thinking about it from her point of view? You know she loves you, right? What else will help you to connect with her point of view?"

Then we are ready to move into the 1 position—we become the new perspective. We are inviting the coachee to experience themselves as if they are the new mindset. The coachee is experiencing being the Realist (Be), experiencing the world of the other (Relate), connected as their future self (Inspire), or as their blue thinker (Think). This 1 position is an important step that follows the 2 position—we are truly embodying the new subpersonality or mindset, speaking as if we are that perspective, thereby embedding it.

Done well, there is a huge power in following these steps—we are allowing the person to move from one mindset to another, one subpersonality to another.

Hints/Tips

It can be helpful to elicit a rich description of the new situation before stepping into it. For example:

Be: Describe the Realist

Relate: Describe the other person (free from your assumption)

Think: Describe a time when you were thinking "blue"

Inspire: Describe a time in the future where you have met your aspirations

In all of these examples, include feelings and thoughts. *Then* invite the coachee to step into this experience in the moment, into the 1 position of the new perspective. Invite the person to talk in the present tense. For example, if challenging an assumption from the Realist, instead of the coachee saying, "The Realist would say the truth is..." invite them to say, "The truth is…." Working in the present in this way really helps to hard-wire the neural pathways of the new perspective.

We are now integrating the new mindset using 3-2-1.

Dimension Five: Practice, practice, practice!

When you watch a butterfly emerging from a cocoon, it first needs to flap its wings and practice flying. This is the same for us as human beings. In coaching, we invite the coachee to experiment.

Through experimentation, the coachee exercises, applies, and builds the muscle of their new worldview or subpersonality. Sometimes we extend the 3-2-1 process to 3-2-1-0. The 0 position is where the coachee is living the new mindsets in their lives. So, we have

3: blind to the new subpersonality or worldview

2: seeing the new subpersonality or worldview

1: being the new subpersonality or worldview

0: living the new subpersonality or worldview

The importance of this can't be understated. Real learning happens through real-life experimenting. A coachee may experience the Realist in a conversation, but the power is when they apply the learning in their real-life circumstances and reflect on that learning to embed the value it brings.

Again, you'll see this featuring in different ways in each of the five conversations.

There are two important moments when it comes to experimenting and action learning.

1. At the end of the conversation, agreeing to specific commitments to experiment. In this part of the conversation, we are inviting the coachee to actively commit to real-life situations where they will bring their learning to life.

Making these experiments tangible and specific will really help. For example, an agreement to experiment tomorrow would not be as strong as agreeing to test the ETC process out in the meeting at 10 a.m., where there is tendency for the coachee to get triggered. The more tangible, the more likely it will occur. In fact, this is where the power of coaching comes to life.

According to the American Psychological Association, the probability of achieving a goal is 10 percent if you hear an idea, 40 percent if you decide to act on it, 50 percent if you make a plan to do it, 65 percent if you commit to someone else that you will act on the plan, and 95 percent if you have a clear accountability meeting with the person you committed to.[8]

2. Following up on the experiments in a future conversation. This is where learning is embedded. Learning both from what worked and what didn't work provides the opportunity for the coachee to reflect and continue to learn. We call this action learning: plan, do, review, and then make sense before planning again. So, once they have reflected, they make a new plan that allows them to continue their experimentation. This brings an acceleration to their learning process.

Coming back to the metaphor of the butterfly, we are really helping the butterfly to flap its wings and become confident in flying. The new subpersonality may not be easy to remember or access. Through action learning, we invite the coachee to remember and learn through practice, building the muscle or hard wiring the new neural pathways through experience.

Hints/Tips

At the end of the conversation, the following questions can be useful:

- What choice do you wish to make now?
- What will you experiment with? How will you apply this into your work/life?

- What opportunities do you have to put this into practice? When will you do it? How will you remember?

It is worth remembering the acronym SMART when creating an experiment: specific, measurable, achievable, realistic, tangible.

In the reflection after the experiment, it is important to remember not to be judgmental as the coach. If the coachee didn't successfully go through it, the coachee can learn as much from their failures as from their success. Here are some questions that help:

- What did you learn?
- How did you feel?
- What's the cost of not doing it? What's the benefit?
- What worked? What didn't work so well? How could you improve next time?
- What will you do differently?
- What was the impact for you, your work, or others around you?
- What stopped you? How can you overcome that next time?

As the coachee progresses with some success, they can choose more and more stretching experiments that really test the muscle of their new perspective.

What stops people from changing?

Four key things can get in the way. We will explore these below, together with some suggestions on how to support our coachees to overcome them.

Barrier One: Don't forget the culture

Barrier:

Sometimes certain subpersonalities are easily activated in certain cultures. For example, your coachee may be working in a proving culture. Things move fast, expectations are high, and employees are tirelessly working long hours with high levels of stress. Even the most centered person is going to be triggered in this type of environment, with their "you must work hard" assumptions enticed to come and play.

Solution:

The important thing is to be conscious of this in your conversations. The awareness will help the coachee be more sensitive of the impact the environment has on them and thereby have more choice in how they respond. For example, a heated exchange in a busy environment might be better resolved if the coachee organized the meeting in a neutral environment. Or if the environment contrasts too strongly with the coachee's values and preferences, you could ask questions that highlight the choices available to them, including questions about whether they are in the right organization for them. There are benefits and downsides to cultures—understanding these will help coachees to make choices about how to make the most of what is valuable and make the right choices with what is not.[9]

For example, a team leader was trying to work on the Think conversation. We agreed on certain experiments for her to explore how to restructure the team so that they could increase efficiencies. She was excited about engaging her newfound Curious Investigator subpersonality, the personification of her blue-thinking mindset. But when she returned for our next conversation, she explained that the team was constantly firefighting to meet stakeholder deadlines. She therefore did not have time to step back and ask the questions to create any new possibilities.

She was in a culture of high pressure and fast turnaround. While she recognized the impact that this had on staff stress levels and turnover, she felt that this situation was inhibiting her desire to do some breakthrough thinking with her team.

Once we identified the cultural dimension, she stepped back to see how she could embrace it. Instead of carving out off-site days with the team to step back together, she chose to use the challenges as an opportunity to deploy her Curious Investigator during work. She started calling 30-minute timeouts for her team to stop and step back. In other words, she did some in-the-moment breakthrough thinking and found a way that worked in her culture. In 10 minutes, she listened to all the perspectives of the team and was able to then address the root cause. The team's capacity to work quickly in this culture helped—together, they readdressed their ways of working in order to find a better solution than the way they had been working.

By becoming aware of the culture, she had been able to identify its limitations, while also being able turn the fast thinking and acting quality of the culture into a strength to find new ways of working.

Hints/Tips

The following questions can be helpful:

What in the culture might be getting in the way for you?

What are the strengths of the culture that you can leverage?

What is the narrative in the culture that you are facing? What is helpful and unhelpful about that? How can you turn it into something positive?

Barrier Two: Old behaviors die hard

Barrier:

Try an experiment now. Fold your arms. You will notice that either you will have put your right arm over the left or vice versa. This will be your usual pattern. Without thinking about it, you will do what you have always done.

Now try folding your arms the other way. You may find it a bit awkward at first, or at least it will feel unusual or different. This is what it is like when trying something new.

Without thinking, a coachee will default into old patterns or familiar ways. Some of these have been going on for years. Trying to change an old pattern requires a conscious effort, and it can feel different.

Solution:

What can help is a continual conscious practice, where the coachee makes a commitment to apply their learning in a deliberate way. This is what we have referred to as action learning: experimenting and consciously learning.

Barrier Three: Attachment to a subpersonality

Barrier:

Sometimes a coachee can be attached to a subpersonality or identity that they don't want to let go of. Or they may be uncomfortable taking on a new identity that changes their perception of themselves.

I supported someone who had an attachment to being perceived as tough and challenging. With a history in the Army, this was a subpersonality that may have worked for him in that particular context. It was his winning formula. When it came to winning people over, this subpersonality came to the foreground: directive and challenging was the way. When people reacted, it was their problem, not his, allowing him to keep his identity fixed.

When we looked at the worldview of the subpersonality that believed "toughness and challenge is the way to get results," he just did not want to let it go. It was familiar and safe. He feared letting that perspective go. What other way was there for him?

Solution:

Explore the payoff and cost

So, how can we work with this? Firstly, it helped to look at the payoff and cost of the subpersonality. The payoff clearly was getting things done. The cost was upsetting people along the way, and in the long run inhibiting his desire to get things done.

In doing this, it can help to get some data in the form of, for example, feedback from colleagues or a 360. This is what we did in the coaching. This helped with receiving some truthful messages about his leadership behavior. Furthermore, the comments allowed some reality about the cost when people were given a chance to share their experience. This feedback also helped with creating an openness to let go—he became willing to change.

By exploring the reality of payoff and cost, the coachee can see some truth: the cost often far outweighs the payoff, and they become more open to change.

Test assumptions

Next, testing the assumptions that drove his subpersonality against the real-life experience of practicing the new mindset became a powerful, albeit sometimes slow, pathway to change. We began with a small experiment to see how results changed when he tried to listen before directing.

Consciously build on the positives of the old personality

Finally, we looked at how he could retain what was useful in his original subpersonality. We don't believe you ever get rid of an identity. It is more that you loosen it, and in that process, you are able to be "choice-full" in how you can bring the valuable aspects of it to the fore. His ability to challenge was valuable. Balanced with his learning to listen and understand others, he was able to bring an even better form of leadership to his role.

And sometimes, it can be scary to let go of an old mindset and expand into a new one. It is unfamiliar and unknown. The safer option is to go back to the familiar. We leave you with an excerpt from Marianne Williamson:

> Our deepest fear is not that we are inadequate. Our deepest fear
> is that we are powerful beyond measure. It is our light, not our
> darkness that most frightens us. We ask ourselves, Who am I to be
> brilliant, gorgeous, talented, fabulous?...Your playing small does
> not serve the world. There is nothing enlightened about shrinking
> so that other people won't feel insecure around you. We are all
> meant to shine, as children do....It's not just in some of us; it's in
> everyone. And as we let our own light shine, we unconsciously
> give other people permission to do the same. As we are liberated
> from our own fear, our presence automatically liberates others.[10]

Barrier Four: Our attitude to learning

Barrier:

We have talked about the importance of experimentation and learning
on the job. One of the biggest barriers to experimenting can be the fear
of failure or a fixed mindset. This inhibits the coachee having a learning
or growth mindset.[11]

This can be worked with, of course, using the Be conversation. Often
you will find in-the-box assumptions: the coachee fears failure or fears
that they haven't got what it takes.

A love of learning is a successful growth mindset that can help with
experiments. I always remember how my daughter, when she was learning to walk, would laugh each time she fell and then just get up and try
again. In no time at all she had mastered the skill of walking.

Imagine instead, if each time she fell, she was berated or told she
was useless or a failure. Not only would it have hurt her self-esteem, but
the willingness to give it another go would have been inhibited. This is
what people do to themselves as adults—it is common for a coachee to
berate themselves for not getting it right the first time, and then find
themselves giving up very quickly. If they gave themselves a little compassion and returned to their innately human mindset of adventure, they
would have much more likely succeeded in achieving whatever they set
out to achieve. This is a great growth mindset to have.

Solution:

We can talk to the coachee about their attitude toward learning and experimentation, and explore healthy mindsets that they can access in helping them give it a go.

The Be conversation can be very powerful here: we can look at a coachee's triggers that bring the limiting mindsets of the pessimistic or judging self-talk about experimenting and learning to the surface of conscious awareness. Then we can encourage the Realist to challenge those closed-minded assumptions. The coachee can liberate the learner in them, a powerful version of the Realist subpersonality.

Conclusion

Remember, mastery takes time. Mastery is not a goal, but a practice. It is through committed conscious practice that you will grow in coaching each of the great conversations.

We have shared a lot of insights and suggestions in this chapter. We wouldn't expect anyone to use all of them at once. In fact, when we train our coaches in some of these conversations, it takes years of conscious practice, which entails recordings with feedback, preparation, observation, and reflective learning. So, take your time and enjoy the process of learning!

Hopefully, you are drawn to at least a few tips to start experimenting as a coach. You will find that over time, these skills come naturally to you, and you can even in the moment offer some transformational questions without having to go through a series of steps.

As you develop mastery, you can increase your creativity. For example, I once worked with a colleague who was struggling with a strong attack from his pessimistic assumptions that left him in the box for a few days. Rather than engage his Realist, we instead used the Presence Triangle process to step into the three different positions: Self, Pessimist, and Observer. The insights that followed were powerful in helping him to recognize the value of the pessimist when standing in this position. In the observer, he was able to see how he could turn the pessimist from foe to friend next time it was triggered. The valuable aspect of the pessimist had the wisdom to point to the areas that were not going well and needed attention, without fearful and dramatized assumptions about the future. He felt freer.

Through practice we are able to access the skills naturally and responsively—the conversation becomes a dance, unlocking creativity and intuition.

The benefits speak for themselves. One great conversation has the power of changing a life forever. Through our practice we become masterful and truly in service to the others we are coaching and the organizations we work in.

....

Chapter 8

A Lifetime
of Learning

I N THIS BOOK WE'VE focused on the four greatest coaching conversations. These are key to the four most important mindset shifts a coachee can make. If you master coaching these conversations, you will most certainly be one of the most effective coaches you can be. For line managers who coach, these conversations can be both

1. Part of a longer coaching conversation or series of conversations to complement and support the coaching objectives, or
2. An in-the-moment coaching intervention day-to-day.

Each day brings you opportunities where each of the four conversations could be useful. It could be someone triggered by a work problem (Be), a disagreement or difficult interaction (Relate), a lack of clarity on what to do (Inspire), or a challenge that needs solving (Think).

By tuning in to the nature of the issue, you can ask powerful questions with each of the mindset shifts that show up—in the moment. Each conversation can be adapted to the moment. For example, someone is triggered, and they are in the box. They want some support to get out, so you could ask, "OK, how are you? What actually happened? What assumptions are you making? OK, let's get to the facts and truth and see what to do." This simple adaptation of ETC could be very helpful. You can do this with the other conversations too. This way you can truly use the opportunities in the workplace to support your coachees to shift from their limiting mindset to a more expansive mindset. The coachees' day-to-day lives become opportunities to practice and embed the learnings. As we have seen, research shows the power of this for people and organizations. It enables you to empower others to realize their true and unlimited potential.

If the coachee's potential is unlimited, this invites the question: Is there more to these core mindsets? Actually, within our research we find that mindsets continue to expand in each of the four domains of Be, Relate, Inspire, and Think. Human beings never stop evolving and expanding! This has been very exciting insight from our coaching data. In other words, we have found

- The Four Great Conversations continue to be the key areas for leadership development, and
- The mindset within each conversation (Be, Relate, Inspire, and Think) continues to evolve and expand. We have found that for each conversation there are three levels of shift; each one evolves after the previous one.

In this book we've described the Four Conversations or domains. Within each conversation, we have focused on the first or level one mindset shifts within that domain. This is relevant for the majority of people you will coach. But with the three mindsets in each of the Four Conversations, there are twelve shifts in total. It is highly unlikely one individual will master all twelve!

We clearly can't add another eight chapters to explore each of these in turn. And that isn't the purpose of this book. So, pause your coach hat for the rest of this chapter. It won't give you hints and tips as a coach—but it will give you some unique insight about the future possibilities for development, with the intention of being brief yet thorough. It is enough just to follow the essence as the Twelve Shifts form a fascinating map within which to navigate a lifetime of leadership development.

Here is the map in its totality:

Figure 8-1- The Twelve Shifts

Let's explore the levels in each domain of the four conversations

We'll explore each with hypothetical examples.

Levels within the Be conversation

Level One: I can choose my attitude

Let's take our imaginary coachee, Alex. Alex is promoted into a big role early on after university. He struggles with confidence and tends to hold back when he's with senior people or more dominant characters. Using the ETC process, he is able to master this. Because of this, he learns to project confidence and be at his best in key situations. This plays a big part in progressing his career.

By mastering Be level one, Alex can respond calmly, empathetically, and confidently when he most needs it.

Level Two: I can be all of me

Ten years later Alex is in a senior position. He is proud of the fact that he no longer holds back and is confident and articulate. But he starts getting feedback that others don't find him fully authentic—he is not showing up as himself, sometimes only projecting confidence. He also realizes that he hides certain aspects of himself and does not truly show up. He is now ready for a level two Be shift.

In making this shift he will learn to accept and integrate all elements of his personality. He will be much more comfortable showing weakness and allowing others to support him. He will find a way to project a leadership personality that is not just confident but authentically him and so much more inspiring for it.

By mastering Be level two, Alex can finally accept and show up as himself. The shift is "I can be all of me." This means he will be more authentic and comfortable in his own skin. He will be aware of his unintended impact and open to learning from it. He is integrating his shadow and light as a leader, exploring how he can turn the volume up on his strengths and find the gift in his shadow.

Level Three: I am an agent for the whole

As he grows, the level three shift may become relevant.

This is a further expansion toward being present to himself and the system he is in, and thereby being more in service to others and the organization.

Levels within the Relate conversation

Level One: I can experience other people's worlds

Let's imagine Rachel. Rachel is a team leader in a tech business. A couple of years into her team leadership she begins to notice that she is less effective with certain team members than others—and also has a new line manager she finds it hard to build trust with. She wrestles with this and realizes that her current gentle style isn't working with these characters. She had to learn what works for them and experiment with more direct communication styles that aren't as comfortable for her. She shifts her approach and quickly sees results. This is the level one Relate shift—the one we've been learning to coach.

The level one shift, using See-Hear-Speak, will typically help Rachel influence others, build relationships and empathize, have a challenging conversation, motivate her team, and adjust her coaching style to those in her team.

Level Two: I am willing to let go and trust

After mastering this, Rachel's career blossoms and she becomes known for her ability to engage others. But many years later her business is acquired. She finds herself co-leading a function with a colleague from the acquiring business. Trust is low, and conflict results with significant power play and politics. However much she tries to understand others, she can't find a way of getting them on board. A new shift is now required.

Rachel needs to expand her mindset: she now sees how she co-creates the relationship dynamics that impact trust. She sees how conflict is an opportunity to show her vulnerability, and thereby break the dynamics and deepen the trust in relationship so that she can let go.

If she can master level two, Rachel will find herself more confident embracing conflict, building even deeper relationships, coaching and empowering others to step into their leadership, and collaborating across the business.

Level Three: Dynamics go beyond me and you

Much later in her leadership career Rachel finds herself in a senior role in which she needs to shape culture and dynamics across a wider system. The level two mindset isn't enough. The level three shift may become important.

Rachel's mindset expands further. She now sees that relationships between individuals and groups are not isolated to these people. They are mirrors of patterns that occur within and beyond the organization. She sees that stress within her organization is connected to the wider economic and political climate.

It is worth highlighting that as the coachee moves through each level, the mindset "expands"—their worldview embraces more perspectives and therefore has greater capacity for impact, and they can deal with greater complexity.

Levels within the Inspire conversation

Level One: I know what I am leading for

Let's take Carol. Carol spends the first five years of her career smashing her sales targets. After two years she is given a team of reps and expects them to do the same. Unfortunately, they aren't as driven, and the team lacks direction and focus. With coaching, Carol uses the ICE process to develop a vision for herself and her team that is much more balanced.

By mastering Inspire level one, Carol knows who she wants to be and the difference she wants to make. This enables her to set a direction for her team and lead them to develop new and more effective ways of selling.

Level Two: I am clear on the difference I want to make

After seven years, she is given the challenge of a big new leadership role in a bank that has suffered from sales scandals. She needs to win back trust in the market. But the team she leads is full of cynicism. Her early attempts to communicate a vision go nowhere.

She is forced to look deeper and find a sense of purpose that speaks to herself and the new team—and to lead change around this. By mastering Inspire level two, Carol is now in a position to shape more complex changes, helping a disillusioned team to find a new sense of purpose. This shift is about getting clear on our meaning and purpose.

Level Three: I am clear why we are here

As she grows, the level three shift may become relevant. This will allow her to shape a purpose that aligns different communities inside and outside the organization—this shift is about moving beyond your own purpose and towards a greater purpose that others can engage with. She will be leveraging her power for societal change.

Levels within the Think conversation

Level One: I act on the whole not the parts

Again, let's take a hypothetical coachee, Alan.

Alan is the shift leader in a factory. He is constantly frustrated by the quality of handovers between shifts. But every idea he tries doesn't seem to improve it. After coaching, he realizes that he needs to step back and see the big picture, getting perspectives from all the key stakeholders. He comes up with a great solution and also becomes sought after in the plant as a great one to consult with on tricky problems.

By mastering Think level one, Alan becomes good at taking a step back, seeing the whole picture, seeking input from multiple perspectives, and synthesizing this into a breakthrough idea.

Level Two: I am seeking new paths

But five years later the business is under pressure. Competitors are creating alternative products that are cheaper and more effective. As plant manager, Alan is challenged by the business to find a response. But this requires more than thinking differently about a problem.

At first, he holds back, knowing his expertise is in short supply and that others know more about the market. Eventually, with coaching, Alan expands the embrace of his curiosity. He encourages his leadership team to get really curious about other industries, and about unrelated digital innovations. Eventually they come up with an insight that reinvents the way they think about their plant.

To master Think level two, Alan has to let go of his need to be an expert. He needs to become a rookie again and get curious about areas he's never even looked at before. This enables him to respond to the radical disruption his business is facing. This shift is more innovating, impactful, and disruptive—and requires navigating greater complexity to generate insight.

Level Three: There is insight in the paradox

As he grows the level three shift may become relevant. This will be particularly true if he takes on a big, complex role in an uncertain context full of "impossible" trade-offs. Level three will help him find the insight in the paradoxes and reframe the way the organization sees itself to unlock new strategic possibilities.

Some key insights when thinking about levels

When we looked into our coaching data, we found

1. Within each domain—Be, Relate, Think, and Inspire—the shifts need to be made in turn.

- Each level transcends and includes the previous level: a coachee embarking on level two will have achieved a shift at level one. (How they do it varies—e.g., through coaching, life experience, or other development intervention—but they can't go to level two without level one).

- These stages are not linear, but can be seen as waves, with the next wave appearing after the previous wave has been developed.

- A coachee may revert back to a previous wave depending on circumstances, but will not skip a level in their vertical development.

2. Across domains leaders can be at different levels.

- Within an area the shifts are sequential, but this is not true across them. You may find a senior leader who is at level three in Think but who struggles with level one in Be. Mastery seems to operate within rather than across domains.

3. The most senior people aren't the most mature.

- Whilst the most senior people aren't always the most mature, there is a correlation between seniority and level. This is because the 12 shifts represent people evolving to more mature worldviews. This can only happen with time and experience.

So, for example, the data created with Singapore Management University[1] shows:

	First-line leaders	Mid-level leaders	Senior leaders
Level One Be (resilience)	24%	23%	18%
Level One Relate (empathy shift)	39%	26%	7%
Level Two Be (crisis of authenticity)	1%	3%	18%
Level Two Relate (crisis of control)	8%	8%	19%
Other (e.g., Think and Inspire shifts)	28%	38%	39%

In other words, level two Relate becomes 19 percent in senior leaders and only 8 percent in first-line leaders; similarly, level two Be is encountered in 18 percent of senior leaders and only 1 percent of first-line leaders.

So, there is undoubtedly a correlation between seniority and level of shift. If you are coaching junior leaders or mid-level leaders, the four conversations we've shared are likely to be of value most of the time.

Of course, this is far from exact. People don't learn at the same rate, and they don't learn in a balanced way. For example, there are plenty of C-suite leaders who are struggling with the level one shifts in our data. One of the real dangers in stereotyping level with need is that we miss this. We often assume there is a correlation between promotion/seniority and mastery. This isn't true, and we all probably know experienced leaders who, while they may be quite brilliant at the Think dimension, still operate at the level of self-awareness that is associated with level one Be, Relate, or Inspire shifts. And of course, we know other leaders whose strengths and weaknesses are the other way around. Because people are immensely different and develop at different rates, it is impossible to generalize.

Perhaps for this reason a number of recent writers have moved from defining "great leadership" in behavioral terms to saying that what is really important is learning agility—the ability to learn and constantly adapt and grow.

So, what is going on here? Vertical development

From our research, we have seen that coachees evolve through stages of development. Before a coachee is ready for a level-two shift in any one quadrant, they will first have achieved awareness and a degree of mastery at level one in that same quadrant.

We see leadership development as a lifelong journey. And as a coaching business we work with any shift that is most relevant for a coachee in any given time. We support the transition through the shift through our insight-led and transformational approach to coaching.

Our experience and research has shown that as a coachee moves through levels one to three, there is an expansion in perspective or worldview—they see more, access more possibility, and widen their embrace in making choices. For example, at level one Inspire, the shift in worldview is about a coachee getting clear on their own values and the vision they wish to create based on these core values. Moving to level three Inspire, the shift has to do with creating a shared purpose that touches the hearts and minds of people in and beyond their organization, expanding their own thinking from individual to the whole system. This worldview is more expanded in its embrace.

This thinking isn't unique. This idea of leaders developing new mindsets as they learn is known more broadly as vertical development. Vertical development entails a growth or expansion in perspective (as opposed to horizontal development, which we define as developing skills and capabilities within our current perspective or worldview).

It is worth mentioning from the outset that developmental theorists throughout history have outlined stages of development that human beings evolve through. Starting at infancy, psychologists from Piaget and Freud to Fowler and Maslow have mapped these stages through observation and research. Seen as one of the greatest philosophers of our time, Ken Wilber has correlated the research from the greatest development psychologists throughout history and shown that they significantly align in their stages of development from childhood to mature adult. His work shows that development never stops. Development and expansion continue throughout life.[2]

Through each stage of development, our outlook or worldview goes through a series of transformational changes. For example, a two-year-old child will look at the world through the lens that they are the center of the universe. This view transforms as the child grows. By the age of five or six they will appreciate that there are others who have different needs and perceptions from theirs, and a recognition that they are not the only participants in their world. This kind of developmental path is also true of adults: there are changes in outlook that continually transform perspectives and the way the world is perceived.

Wilber offers an essential view of these stages of development, describing them as colors on a spectrum that we move through as we grow and develop.[3] We include the stages relevant to this book:

Red: This stage is egocentric and protective. It aligns with Piaget's pre-operational thinking, Fowler's mythic-literal stage, and Maslow's survival stage. A person at this stage will be concerned about their needs, looking at the world to satisfy their own personal drives and goals, with limited capacity to take the role of the other.

Amber: This stage is ethnocentric—the person has now expanded their concern beyond themself to the group and now favors their group above all others, aligning with Maslow's belonging stage and Piaget's concrete operational thinking.

Orange: At this world-centric stage, the person moves away from identification with the group (family, religion, or nation) and becomes more of a citizen of the world. This stage is rational and conscientious and aligns with Piaget's formal operational thinking, Fowler's individual-reflective, and Maslow's self-esteem stage. This stage is the goal of our Western educational system, and the transition to this stage most often occurs between adolescence and early adulthood.

Green: A person at this stage is moving beyond world-centric, developing in compassion, and may include a significant social responsibility in their perspective. This aligns with Maslow's self-actualization stage and Fowler's conjunctive faith level.

After **Green**, we have **Teal** (Kosmocentric), **Turquoise**, **Indigo,** and **Violet**—through these states there is even further expansion in perspective. **Teal** and **Turquoise** correspond to Fowler's universalizing faith level and Maslow's self-actualization and self-transcendence stages.

Note:

1. These stages are not hierarchical in that one is better than the other. For example, no one would argue that an adolescent is better than an infant. However, with greater development comes greater capacity for perspective and impact.

2. Many people do not move significantly beyond the orange stage in the Western world and will plateau at a stage that is at the center of gravity of the culture they are in.

3. Wilber estimates that approximately 66 percent of the world's population operate at amber or below stage of consciousness (which is corroborated in our research).

The important message to recognize here is that vertical development continues throughout our lives. Horizontal development is an expansion of capacities at a particular level, while vertical development is an expansion in perspective. How does this relate to leadership and our 12 shifts framework?

Bill Torbert, through his research with leaders, created the Leadership Development Framework. He showed similarly that leaders go through a series of development stages, which he called action logics—these action logics align with the stages above: the Opportunist (corresponding to red), the Diplomat (corresponding to amber), the Expert and Achiever (corresponding to orange), the Individualist (corresponding to green), the Strategist (corresponding to teal), and so forth.[4] While the description of these action logics is outside the scope of this work, the work of Torbert and his associates corroborates vertical development in leadership and shows the greater impact of vertical development in leadership.

In their paper in the *Harvard Business Review,* they found that of the 10 CEOs of six companies, five of the CEOs were measured at the Strategist level and five were measured at other action logics. Of the five Strategists, all had successfully implemented organizational transformations in a period of four years, where the company's profitability, market share, and reputation all improved. For the other CEOs, only two succeeded in doing the same.[5]

Further work at Harvard was done by Suzanne Cook-Greuter. She undertook a 20-year research study on ego maturity and leadership, with an extensive sample size of over 5,000 leaders. Once again, her model corresponded with Torbert and Wilber. Her research confirmed that 85 percent of her sample were seen to be at the Achiever stage or below, while approximately 12 percent were at Individualist and Strategist stages, and fewer than 3 percent were at the stages beyond.[6] This data is also approximately reflected in our own research of clients that we coached.

P. Williams and D. Menendez refer to Robert Kegan, a retired professor at Harvard University, whose development model is in agreement with Wilber, Torbert, and Cook-Greuter:

> Robert Kegan is one of the foremost researchers to have developed a theory of human development.... [An] essential principle of Kegan's work is that movement from stage to stage of development is really about a transformation. It does not happen all at once. Transformation may take years to unfold.... [W]hen shifts do occur, they are always associated with the emergence of significant new capability. Research also shows that people seldom regress permanently to a previous level, although they can regress temporarily under stress or trauma. The new order of consciousness transcends the limits of the old order and is better matched to the demands of the world the client now inhabits. It simply works better.[7]

These transformations in consciousness align with the shifts in our 12 shifts framework, specifically with the orange-to-teal transformations. Our shifts at the three levels support the transformations in consciousness that allow the leader to move through these particular stages of development, as shown in the table below:

Twelve Shifts Framework Stages	Wilber Stages	Torbert Stages
Level one shifts	**Amber** to **Orange**	Expert to Achiever
Level two shifts	**Orange** to **Green**	Achiever to Individualist
Level three shifts	**Green** to **Teal**	Individualist to Strategist

The majority of our coaching work occurs at levels one and two, aligning with Cook-Greuter's research that 85 percent of the leaders she interviewed were at Achiever stage of development or below. Our coaching supports the vertical development of leaders, giving leaders an opportunity to transform in their worldview to have greater perspective, choice, freedom, and power to influence wider change and impact.

So what insights do the 12 shifts bring?

Many vertical development theorists talk about generic levels. You are at an "Orange" stage or at a "Green" stage.

But we have seen that mindset change isn't so simple. People aren't at one level or another. They can be flying in Think and really stuck at level one in Be.

This is exciting. It means that we have here a holistic map of human development. At any stage in our life, one of the 12 shifts is likely to predominate. It will be the place we can learn. We can choose where to spend our time and effort.

And more than this, by getting specific we can target the right coaching conversation at the right shift. In this book we've explored the big four—the four greatest conversations that unlock the level one mindset shifts. As you've seen, this is over 85 percent of conversations. But there are equally important conversations that unlock the level two shifts, and that support level three coaching.

But that is probably the subject for another book. Enjoy the process of the lifelong journey!

References

Introduction

1. Saumya Sindhwani, Jerry Connor, and Howard Thomas, "Exposed and Under Pressure," *Asian Management Insights* 4, no. 2 (2017): 32–37.
2. Saumya Sindhwani, Jerry Connor, and Howard Thomas, "The Missing Shifts," *EFMD Global Focus* 1, no. 13 (2019), https://media.globalfocus magazine.com/wp-content/uploads/2019/02/01163244/Issue_1_2019_The _missing_shifts.pdf.
3. R. Kegan and L. L. Lahey, *Immunity to Change: How to Overcome It and Unlock Potential in Yourself and Your Organization* (Boston: Harvard Business Press, 2009).
4. Jeff Fermin, "Statistics on the Importance of Employee Feedback," *Officevibe*, 7 October 2014, https://www.officevibe.com/blog/infographic -employee-feedback.
5. A. J. Crum, P. Salovey, and S. Achor, "Rethinking Stress: The Role of Mindsets in Determining the Stress Response," *Journal of Personality and Social Psychology* 104, no. 4 (2013): 716–733.
6. A. B. Frymier and M. K. Nadler, *Persuasion: Integrating Theory, Research, and Practice, 4th Edition* (Dubuque: Kendall Hunt Publishing, 2017).

Chapter 1

1. A. Mehrabian and S. R. Ferris, "Inference of Attitudes from Nonverbal Communication in Two Channels," *Journal of Consulting Psychology* 31, no. 3 (1967): 48–258.

A. Mehrabian and M. Wiener, "Decoding of Inconsistent Communications," *Journal of Personality and Social Psychology* 6 (1967): 109–114.

2. D. Goleman, *Emotional Intelligence* (London: Bloomsbury Publishing Plc., 1996).

3. K. Neff, *Self-Compassion: Stop Beating Yourself Up and Leave Insecurity Behind* (London: Hodder and Stoughton, 2011).

4. A. McKee, C. Congleton, D. Goleman, and E. Langer, *Harvard Business Review Emotional Intelligence Collection* (Boston: Harvard Business School Publishing Corporation, 2017).

5. meQuilibrium, "The Science Behind Resilience," *New Life Solutions*, 2015, https://www.mequilibrium.com/wp-content/uploads/2016/01/The -Science-Behind-Resilience-12-22.pdf.

6. M. Cerf, "Neuroscientists Have Identified How Exactly a Deep Breath Changes Your Mind," *Quartzy*, November 19, 2017, https://qz.com/ quartzy/1132986.

Chapter 2

1. W. A. Gentry, T. J. Weber, and G. Sadri, "Empathy in the Workplace: A White Paper," *Center for Creative Leadership*, 2007, https://www.ccl.org/ wp--content/uploads/2015/04/EmpathyInTheWorkplace.pdf.

2. R. Praszkier, "Empathy, Mirror Neurons and SYNC," *Mind and Society* 15 (December 14, 2014).

3. V. Kolmannskog, *The Empty Chair: Tales from Gestalt Therapy* (London: Routledge, Taylor & Francis Group, 2018).

4. T. Hoobyar, T. Dotz, and S. Sanders, *NLP: The Essential Guide to Neuro-Linguistic Programming* (New York: HarperCollins, 2013).

5. J. S. Beck and A. T. Beck, *Cognitive Behavior Therapy* (New York: The Guilford Press, 2011).

6. C. Otto Scharmer, *Theory U: Leading from the Future as It Emerges* (Oakland: Berrett-Koehler Publishers, Inc., 2007).

7. R. Boyatzis, A. Passarellia, K. Koenig, M. Lowe, B. Mathew, J. K. Stoller, and M. Phillips, "Examination of the Neural Substrates Activated in Memories of Experiences with Resonant and Dissonant Leaders," *The Leadership Quarterly* 23, no. 2 (2012): 259–272.

8. T. Bartram and G. Casimir, "The Relationship between Leadership and Follower In-Role Performance and Satisfaction with the Leader: The Mediating Effects of Empowerment and Trust in the Leader," *Leadership & Organization Development Journal* 28, no. 1 (2007): 4–19.

9. F. Lee, A. Edmondson, S. Thomke, and M. Worline, "The Mixed Effects of Inconsistency on Experimentation in Organizations," *Organization Science* 15, no. 3 (2004): 310–326.

10. L. Norman, N. Lawrence, A. Iles, A. Benattayallah, and A. Karl, "Attachment-Security Priming Attenuates Amygdala Activation to Social and Linguistic Threat," *Social Cognitive and Affective Neuroscience* 10, no. 6 (October 17, 2014): https://doi.org/10.1093/scan/nsu127.

11. "UK Workers Value Culture and Recognition over Pay *HR Magazine*, 14 July 2014, https://www.hrmagazine.co.uk/article-details/uk-workers-value-culture-and-recognition-over-pay-survey-finds.

12. "Gallup Releases New Findings on the State of the American Workplace," *Gallup*, June 11, 2013, https://news.gallup.com/opinion/gallup/170570/gallup-releases-new-findings-state-american-workplace.aspx.

13. K. Dirks and D. Ferrin, "Trust in Leadership: Meta-Analytic Findings and Implications for Research and Practice," *Journal of Applied Psychology* 87, no. 4 (2002): 611–628.

14. S. G. Barsdale and O. A. O'Neill, "What's Love Got to Do with It? A Care Setting," *Administrative Science Quarterly* 59, no. 4 (2014): 551–598.

15. E. D. Heaphy and J. E. Dutton, "Positive Social Interactions and the Human Body at Work: Linking Organizations and Physiology," *Academy of Management Review* 33, no. 1 (2008): 137–162.

16. D. Goleman, R. Boyatzis, and A. McKee, *Primal Leadership: Realizing the Power of Emotional Intelligence* (Boston: Harvard Business School Press, 2002).

17. D. Goleman, *Emotional Intelligence* (London: Bloomsbury Publishing Plc., 1996).

18. S. Heen and D. Stone, *Thanks for the Feedback: The Science and Art of Receiving Feedback Well* (New York: Portfolio Penguin, 2015).

Chapter 3

1. R. McGough, "The Leader Poem," in *All the Best: The Selected Poems of Roger McGough* (London: Penguin, 2003).

2. Dyson Corporation, "About James Dyson," https://www.dyson.com.au/community/about-james-dyson.aspx.

3. University of Notre Dame, "The Hesburgh-Yusko Scholars Program," https://hesburgh-yusko.nd.edu/assets/172346/28009_hysp_tri.pdf.

4. J. Ryan, "Leadership Success Always Starts with Vision," *Forbes*, July 29, 2009, https://www.forbes.com/2009/07/29/personal-success-vision-leadership-managing-ccl.html#37ab445e6634.

5. *The Times of India*, January 23, 2013, https://www.youtube.com/watch?v=V-gvE7MGIBw.

6. R. Fritz, *The Path of Least Resistance* (New York: Fawcett Columbine, 1989).

7. K. Dirks and D. Ferrin, "Trust in Leadership: Meta-Analytic Findings and Implications for Research and Practice." *Journal of Applied Psychology* 87, no. 4 (2002): 611–628.

8. C. Poulton, C. N. G. Proches, and R. Sibanda, "The Impact of Value Systems on the Development of Effective Leadership," *International Business Management* 11 (2017): 8–10.

9. R. Barrett, *The Values-Driven Organization* (London: Routledge, 2014).

10. R. Nadler, "Steve Jobs: Superman Syndrome, Low EQ, High IQ," *Psychology Today*, November 16, 2011, https://www.psychologytoday.com/gb/blog/leading-emotional-intelligence/201111/steve-jobs-superman-syndrome-low-eq-high-iq.

11. J. H. Zenger and J. Folkman, *The Extraordinary Leader: Turning Good Managers into Great Leaders* (New York: McGraw Hill, 2002).

Chapter 4

1. S. R. Covey, *The 7 Habits of Highly Effective People* (New York: Free Press, 2004).

2. Dyson Corporation, "About James Dyson," https://www.dyson.com.au/community/about-james-dyson.aspx.

3. J. Dyer, H. Gregersen, and C. M. Christensen, "*The Innovator's DNA*" (Boston: Harvard Business School Publishing, 2011).

4. E. Weisskopf-Joelson and T. S. Eliseo, "An Experimental Study of Brainstorming," *Journal of Applied Psychology* 45, no. 1 (1961).

5. V. John-Steiner, *Notebooks of the Mind* (Albuquerque: University of New Mexico Press, 1985).

6. C. M. Seifert, D. Meyer, N. Davidson, and A. Patalano, "Demystification of Cognitive Insight: Opportunistic Assimilation and the Prepared Mind Perspective," in *The Nature of Insight*, edited by R. J. Sternberg and J. E. Davidson (Cambridge: MIT Press 1985).

7. "Breakthrough Innovation and Growth," *PWC*, 2013, https://www.pwc.co.uk/assets/pdf/achieving-business-growth.pdf.

Chapter 6

1. R. Assagioli, *Transpersonal Development* (Should list city here: Smiling Wisdom, 2007).

2. "Our Heritage," *Starbucks*, https://www.starbucks.co.uk/about-us/our-heritage.

3. D. Goleman, R. Boyatzis, and A. McKee, *Primal Leadership: Realizing the Power of Emotional Intelligence* (Boston: Harvard Business School Press, 2002).

4. P. M. Senge, *The Fifth Discipline: The Art and Practice of the Learning Organization* (London: Random House, 2006).

5. Ibid.

6. J. M. Kouzes and B. Z. Posner, *The Leadership Challenge* (Hoboken: John Wiley and Sons, Inc., 2017)

7. H. Gardner, *Multiple Intelligences* (New York: Basic Books, 2006).

Conclusion

1. See, for example, Zenger and Foldman's 2002 work.

Chapter 7

1. D. M. Eagleman, *Incognito: The Secret Lives of the Brain* (London: Canongate Books Ltd., 2011).

2. *Inside Out*, directed by Pete Docter (Emeryville: Pixar Animation Studios, 2015).

3. A. Storr, *Freud: A Very Short Introduction* (Oxford: Oxford University Press, 1989).

4. A. Korb, *The Upward Spiral* (Vancouver: Raincast Books, 2015).

5. D. Rock, *Your Brain at Work* (New York: HarperCollins, 2009).

6. Korb, *The Upward Spiral*.

7. K. Wilber, *Integral Psychology* (Boston: Shambala Productions, Inc., 2000).

8. S. Fairley and W. M. Zipp, *The Business Coaching Toolkit: Top Ten Strategies for Solving the Toughest Dilemmas Facing Organizations* (Hoboken: John Wiley and Sons, Inc., 2008).

9. J. Connor and L. Sears, *Why Work Is Weird* (London: Marshall Cavendish, 2005).

10. M. Williamson, *A Return to Love* (London: HarperCollins, 1992).

11. C. S. Dweck, *Mindset: The New Psychology of Success* (New York: Ballantine Books, 2008).

Chapter 8

1. S. Sindhwani, J. Connor, and H. Thomas, "The Missing Shifts," *EFMD Global Focus* 1, no. 13 (2019): https://media.globalfocusmagazine.com/wp-content/uploads/2019/02/01163244/Issue_1_2019_The_missing_shifts.pdf.
2. K. Wilber, *Integral Psychology* (Boston: Shambala Productions, Inc., 2000).
3. Ibid.
4. B. Torbert, D. Fisher, and D. Rooke, *Action Inquiry: The Secret of Timely and Transforming Leadership* (Oakland: Berrett-Koehler Publishers, Inc., 2004).
5. D. Rooke and W. R. Torbert, "Seven Transformations of Leadership," *Harvard Business Review,* April 2005, https://hbr.org/2005/04/seven-transformations-of-leadership.
6. S. R. Cook-Greuter, "Ego Development: Nine Levels of Increasing Embrace," 2005, www.cook-greuter.com.
7. P. Williams and D. Menendez, *Becoming a Professional Life Coach* (New York: W.W. Norton and Company, 2007).